# HIP HOP GENIUS

## Remixing High School Education

## Samuel Steinberg Seidel

ROWMAN & LITTLEFIELD EDUCATION

A division of
ROWMAN & LITTLEFIELD PUBLISHERS, INC.
Lanham • New York • Toronto • Plymouth, UK

Published by Rowman & Littlefield Education
A division of Rowman & Littlefield Publishers, Inc.
A wholly owned subsidiary of
The Rowman & Littlefield Publishing Group, Inc.
4501 Forbes Boulevard, Suite 200, Lanham, Maryland 20706
http://www.rowmaneducation.com

Estover Road, Plymouth PL6 7PY, United Kingdom

British Library Cataloguing in Publication Information Available

**Library of Congress Cataloging-in-Publication Data**

The hardback edition of this book was previously cataloged by the Library of
Congress as follows:

Seidel, Samuel Steinberg, 1978-
  Hip hop genius : remixing high school education / Samuel Steinberg Seidel.
    p. cm.
  Includes bibliographical references and index.
  1. High School for Recording Arts (St. Paul, Minn.) 2. Teenagers with
social disabilities—Education (Secondary)—Minnesota—St. Paul.
  3. Hip-hop—Influence. I. Title.
  LD7501.S9246S45 2011
  373.776'581—dc22
                                                          2010052910
ISBN: 978-1-61048-026-0 (cloth : alk. paper)
ISBN: 978-1-61048-027-7 (pbk. : alk. paper)
ISBN: 978-1-61048-028-4 (electronic)

Printed in the United States of America

Royalties received are being donated to
the High School for Recording Arts.

www.hiphopgenius.org

In memory of Jacob Delgado, Matthew Omisore, and Henry Seidel. Three people without whom I could not have written this book. And all of whom I wish I could have shared and discussed it with.

# CONTENTS

# FOREWORD

*George Clinton*

When I was thirteen years old, I heard a song called "Why Do Fools Fall in Love" by Frankie Lymon and the Teenagers. I had just moved to New Jersey and, barely a teenager myself, I was already working at a barbershop. I knew as soon as I heard that song that I wanted to make my living through making music. So I formed a doo-wop group and we practiced around the barbershop. Ten years later, we had our first hit single, "I Wanna Testify" and I have been traveling the universe ever since.

Just like Frankie Lymon inspired me, I have gone on to inspire others. Countless rap records have been made by sampling my songs and sounds, but it doesn't stop there. I've collaborated with some of the most talented hip-hop artists from *all over the country*—from Tupac to Too $hort, from Outkast to Wu Tang. And it isn't just about the music itself. It took a perfect storm to give birth to hip-hop and it was funk's ethos that taught hip-hop the fine art of dancing underwater without getting wet.

Because, like funk, hip-hop is not only a music, it's a way-of-life. For me, it was funk that opened doors to traveling the world, singing, writing, producing, and so many other opportunities. My musical ideas and abilities were my tickets, but funk was the passport. The same can be true for young people; through hip-hop they can discover how to transform one opportunity into the next new thing.

Whenever you hear people say, "That ain't music! That ain't no real music . . ." *That's* gonna be the new music. You can count on that being the new music. Because kids love to do what you don't want them to do. You don't like it . . . *That's what it's gonna be*. Think about it. Feedback on the guitar was noise when I was growing up. Jimi Hendrix made that sucka pleasurable!

That's what *Hip Hop Genius* is. Taking something that everyone else thought was a mistake and making it the next big sensation. Taking what you've already got in your DNA and unlocking it to make your circumstances into something infinitely better. That's what I've had the chance to do. And so has David "TC" Ellis. He's done his job with the school, coming from the streets, kicking it about anything possible. Even when they try to stop his ass. And I know they've tried to stop him. But he's been doing it and he's still doing it and I'm glad to see he's still doing it.

And I'm glad to see the young people at the High School for Recording Arts doing what they do. Every day, these youngsters make the choice to be creative and collaborate in the face of the chaos around them. I know because I've been there.

I've walked through the school and felt the energy. I've been in their recording studio and watched a young man engineer as I stepped to the mic. I've rocked alongside their talented students and staff. I've known TC, the school's founder, since Prince introduced us and we recorded, performed, and appeared in a movie together!

I've seen how unique and transformational the educational model is and how hip-hop is saving lives. Through hip-hop, kids learn ways to count, sequence computers, and do the most involved tasks. Because we learn when we're interested in what we're learning.

If you can find a way to get somebody interested enough to learn, they'll do it themselves. The key is for them to learn how to learn. Not to learn tricks. To learn how to be open to learning. When you learn how to learn, *then* you're able to appreciate things.

So why aren't more people creating schools that understand and value this?

When I was a teenager, I was passionate about music, but that passion had to be fed outside of school. I wish I could have gone to a high school that allowed me to focus on music and entertainment.

Every day, kids are getting struck by a desire to be something, the way I was struck by that Frankie Lymon song. The High School for Recording Arts is one of the few places I've seen that fashions itself to help those young people dive so deep into their dreams that they become their realities.

I wish everyone could visit this school. If you can't make it in person, read this book! I hope it inspires each and every one of you. I want it to spark a movement. Whether it is more schools like the High School for Recording Arts or a whole bunch of different programs coming together, I want to see a nation of talented, confident, creative young leaders rising up.

I'll see you up there!

**George Clinton** is the founder of Parliament, Funkadelic, P-Funk, and Mothers Hip Connection.

# PREFACE

*Herbert Kohl*

**H**ip *Hop Genius* is an exuberant book. It tells the story of the High School for Recording Arts (HSRA) in St. Paul, Minnesota, aka Hip-Hop High, and provides an in-depth portrait of what an effective special public high school can do to allow students, even those with the least successful school careers, to thrive.

The school is centered on the recording arts and hip-hop culture. In particular, hip-hop originated as rap-based music and dance performance in the South Bronx; hip-hop has grown into a cultural movement involving dress, entrepreneurship, and political and social activism— activism on a worldwide scale. Central to hip-hop is respect for the most creative, ingenious, and egalitarian aspects of urban African American youth culture.

Like all other cultural movements that hope to survive and grow, hip-hop culture needs to develop continuity through an education appropriate to the values it espouses. The High School for Recording Arts in St. Paul is a bold and exciting attempt to build a high school rooted in this culture and based on performance, music and video production, community-based learning, the study of urban African American youth culture, and the development of performer and community-controlled businesses. It also attempts to integrate more traditional academic knowledge into its hip-hop focus. But it is resolutely centered on a music production studio, small businesses, and classes designed to analyze the role of African American teenagers in current social, political, and cultural production.

The school was developed by David "TC" Ellis who himself was a struggling student in the St. Paul public schools. According to Sam Seidel, TC "is a great school leader. This statement is true not *despite* the academic struggles he went through as a student, but *because* of them. . . . It has enabled him to understand the broad spectrum of experiences that comprise the realities for students and families at HSRA. TC has built the school to reflect and make room for all of the talents and tragedies students bring through the door each day."

The brilliance of building a school around the recording arts is that the arts draw from a wide range of skills and talents. The entertainment industry employs lawyers; agents; publicists; marketing people; writers, composers, and lyricists; computer, video, and sound technicians; artists and illustrators; accountants and bookkeepers; businesspeople; producers; fundraisers; and set, costume, and rigging designers, as well as musicians and singers. The school is not for young people who want to be hip-hop artists but for students involved in a wide range of vocations who have to learn how to cooperate in order to develop, produce, and market a successful product. It is the kind of place that makes sense to many young African Americans and can lead them to complex learning and productive and profitable work.

The idea of a school for the recording arts takes the notion of having special arts, drama, music, and science high schools to a different level, with an enlarged vision of centering the school about an industry, not a particular aspect of it, such as performance.

A hip-hop school, such as HSRA, should not be mistaken for an Afrocentric school, though it is centered on certain aspects of contemporary African American and young people's culture. It is also not a school centered on black studies. It is basically an outpost for the development of hip-hop culture, for the active expression of what Sam Seidel calls Hip Hop Genius.

The High School for Recording Arts does not fit into models encouraged or mandated by No Child Left Behind or Race to the Top, but it does serve students who will not let themselves be left behind and are certainly running a race to the top, albeit on another path or maybe on a different mountain than that conceived of by politicians or educational professionals.

It is heartening to see such schools as HSRA emerging in the current educational climate. It reminds me of the sixties when, in the midst of a previous rigid-test-oriented era in public education, a number of decent schools that created more effective and student-oriented ways of edu cating high school students, such as Other Ways in Berkeley (where I was the director), the Group School in Cambridge, Independence High School in Newark, and the St. Paul Open School in St. Paul, were created. Ironically enough, David "TC" Ellis graduated from the St. Paul Open School.

The schools thrived for a while and then funding problems, political resistance from public school authorities, and at times just plain fatigue defeated or deflated most of them. All of these schools were willing to conform to the minimal requirements of obtaining public funding, such as some testing, legal responsibility, and evaluating and reporting their work to the school district. But they resisted attempts to rip their hearts out and become rigid, test-obsessed institutions.

Not surprisingly, HSRA is under similar pressure—as are other public high schools such as the El Puente Academy for Peace and Justice in Brooklyn. They always face the threat of being defunded since they do not fit the mold of the standards- and test-driven schools whose performance, when simplified and trivialized, can be summarized by test scores that can be used for national comparisons.

This book, in additional to making a strong case for the ideas driving HSRA, provides a powerful and vivid portrait of the workings of the school, of some of its students, and of the contents and specifics of activity at the school. It illustrates what students do, how they relate to the staff, how the curriculum is developed, and how decision making is distributed throughout all members of the school community. It also provides a history of the development of the school and its charismatic leader.

Now that HSRA and other schools that, like it, refuse to fit into a uniform model of the way high schools should work and how young people must be forced to learn are under siege, a book like *Hip Hop Genius* is a weapon for the defense of the resilience, brilliance, and strengths of young people and for schools designed to serve them. I wish we had had such a book as a weapon for our self-defense during the struggles of the sixties. It provides evidence for the way in which diversity in schooling can overcome intractable problems of public education and should be used in defense of democratic, wider ranging schooling. The educational establishment is cynically obsessed with one-way schooling, and this book is a call for resistance and opposition through the power of the portrait it provides of what creative education looks like.

**Herbert Kohl** continues to teach. He is author of *36 Children*, *I Won't Learn from You*, and *The Discipline of Hope*, as well as other books on education.

# INTRODUCTION

A TV satellite dish made of tin cans. A tattoo gun crafted out of a ballpoint pen and rubber bands. Turntables and speakers plugged into a streetlamp to power music for a block party. Cueing two records up to the same point and switching back and forth to extend dancers' favorite segments of songs. A high school dropout, turned graduate, turned drug addict, turned rapper, starting a school out of a recording studio . . .

These images exemplify *Hip Hop Genius*—creative resourcefulness in the face of limited resources. Or as it is often said in the hip-hop community: flipping something outta nothing. In the context of a dismal national economy and an education system that abandons millions, particularly black and Latino students and students from low- and no-income families, this concept holds much-needed solutions.

The term *Hip Hop Genius* was coined in 2005, when Isaac Ewell brought together a group of educators who were all hip-hop lovers concerned about the national dropout epidemic. Ewell had recently been hired as the director of the Black Alliance for Educational Options Small Schools Initiative.

In his work to support the formation of a network of secondary schools that provide high-quality choices for black students, Ewell had learned about a school in St. Paul, Minnesota, with an unusual model that was yielding promising results: the High School for Recording Arts (HSRA). Ewell was inspired by his first experiences at the school and invited several of us to join him on a subsequent trip.

"In HSRA I saw a school that could reach and retain the young people that few other schools wanted or knew how to serve," Ewell reflects on his first visit. Over the last six years, through his work with the Black Alliance for Educational Options, Ewell has stewarded grants to schools that provide highly structured programs for kids from the 'hood, such as the Boys' Latin of Philadelphia Charter School, where all students wear uniforms and study Latin, and many participate in extracurricular activities such as choir and a rowing team.

Boys' Latin has shown most every kind of success that can be demonstrated by a new school. But, while thrilled with the school's accomplishments, Ewell acknowledges that these environments are not the best match for every student. "There's no one-size-fits-all solution," Ewell explains, adding that he believes he would have thrived at a school like HSRA.

"If we are serious about all kids succeeding, we really need a menu of options. Think about the cats who are really *really* struggling," Ewell pushes, "who maybe don't have anyone at home helping them get that tie on and out the door each morning? Who are having trouble figuring out how to be true to themselves and their community and at the same time be a successful and beneficial member of society?"

The young people Ewell is concerned about serving are not an anomaly in this country. Nationally, 1.23 million high school students are projected to leave school without a diploma this year.[1] Some are expelled, some more subtly encouraged to disappear, and some depart to pursue jobs, take care of children, or because school has been a painful place. These numbers are far worse for black, Latino, and Native American students; those whose families are poor; lesbian, gay, bisexual, and transgender young people; males; and those in urban schools.[2]

Although *Time* magazine hadn't yet declared on its cover that we were living in a "dropout nation," the group Ewell assembled at HSRA in 2005 already knew that our country was in a moment of crisis. He asked the six of us to consider the implications of HSRA's design in addressing the national education opportunity gap, especially as it affected young black men.

Students led us on a tour of the school, showing us the physical design and explaining how the institution functioned. At the end of the tour, one of the students, Devon Johnson, handed out business cards for his music production company and played us a few beats he had made. Impressed by the quality of Johnson's production and engineering, and always on the lookout for hot beats, I asked him if I could buy one of the instrumentals.

"No," he replied. "But we could make an arrangement whereby I'd license it to you for specific uses," he quickly added, explaining why he refused to sell his beats and pulling a two-page licensing contract from his folder. The group was blown away by Johnson's business savvy and how seamlessly it seemed to be integrated with his musical prowess.

Our hosts, HSRA's founder David "TC" Ellis and director of development Tony Simmons, described the school's origins and program design and shared stories of successes and challenges they had faced over the years. Fanon Wilkins, a professor of African American history and culture, probed the philosophical underpinnings of the school's approach and drew connections to black arts and social movements.

Having directed a community-based youth program that was an incubator for young hip-hop artists and leaders, I recognized and highlighted the possibilities that occur when students are engaged not as consumers but as creators. Drawing on his experiences launching after-school tutoring companies, education entrepreneur Jason Green sparked a discussion of the scalability of the school's programs. Collectively we reflected on the global achievements of hip-hop culture and the devastating irony that the very demographics of young people who created it were being left behind.

Each of us had experience bringing hip-hop music and culture into our work as educators and was familiar with hip-hop-related educational approaches being implemented in various schools and programs around the country. We agreed that most of what we had done and seen was too literal and too literary. That is to say, hip-hop education had largely been viewed as classroom lessons focused on the texts of rap music.

While we had experienced and witnessed successes doing such work, we recognized its limitations: it often kept teachers in a position of authority—a peculiar position when studying something of which students often have more knowledge than their instructors; it generally occurred within traditional institutions that many young people found alienating; it privileged rap music over all other manifestations of hip-hop culture; and it often kept students in the position of consumers rather than creators of cultural products.

We also acknowledged that while we all identified hip-hop as a guiding cultural force in our lives, current students might choose to identify differently. For all of these reasons, we found ourselves drawn not just to the recording studios and overt study of hip-hop occurring at HSRA but to the more metaphorical manners in which the school embodied what we perceived to be hip-hop's essence.

In his essay "Dezyne Klass: Exploring Image-Making through the Visual Culture of Hip Hop," John Jennings, a friend of Fanon Wilkins and an associate professor of graphic design at the University of Illinois, shares his definition of hip-hop aesthetics. He suggests that due to the stark societal situations from which hip-hop emerged, it was a culture "forged in improvisation, pain, and a hope for better things."[3] Therefore, "Hip hop was about taking nothing and making something. Its creators used what was present in their postmodern and seemingly dystopian environment and created a phenomenon."[4]

Chicagoan emcee Lupe Fiasco perfectly captures this sentiment in one line of a rap song: "I back-flipped on the mattress they slept on me on."[5] Here is a young man who feels unnoticed, who has been "slept on" by those who should have recognized his talent. Instead of shuffling off quietly, he takes an object that represents the public's doubt in him and literally flips on it, committing an act of physical agility, a staple of breakdancing always sure to wow a crowd.[6]

In the 1970s, Lupe Fiasco's hip-hop predecessors in the predominantly black and Latino community of the South Bronx saw jobs disappear en masse as the area suffered from wounds inflicted by New York City's government, which had sliced through the borough to insert a highway for suburban commuters. From underfunded schools and social services to the destruction of buildings, parks, and streets for the construction of the Cross Bronx Expressway, New York City's government was, at best, neglecting and, at worst, deliberately destroying the neighborhood. Robert Caro—who wrote an exhaustive biography of Robert Moses, the urban planner responsible for the expressway—posits that Moses had a history of racist actions and intentionally sent the road through the South Bronx to damage the community, when there was a more direct route just below the neighborhood.[7]

In *Can't Stop Won't Stop: A History of the Hip-Hop Generation*, Jeff Chang breaks down the math on the exodus of jobs from the South Bronx around this time and concludes: "If blues culture had developed under the conditions of oppressive, forced labor, hip-hop culture would arise from the conditions of no work."[8] It was not a coincidence that, in the face of such racially charged economic challenges and alienation from the city's power structure, young people found the inspiration and ambition to splice wires into streetlamps, tapping the municipal grid to siphon electricity for community celebrations. Or that, in an exercise of similar bravado, young people in the same circumstances took preexisting recordings—some famous and some obscure—and manipulated them to make new music.

Artists in all genres have played and modified others' compositions; but it's another, bolder thing to chop them up and distort them by literally pulling the record backwards on a turntable to make a totally different sound. In each of these instances, there's a technical innovation (converting the voltage of a streetlight to the voltage needed for speakers or wiring turntables to fade sound back and forth), but the technical know-how is only useful if you have the imagination, desire, and confidence to do something that's never been done.

As innovations emerge, societal systems respond to repress and co-opt actions that threaten the status quo. But resourceful creativity continues. Graffiti artists engaged in "reverse colonization," sneaking into train yards and re-appropriating subway cars as mobile canvases.[9] They did not need representation from galleries to have their artwork seen. They painted trains and instantly had audiences all over the city. When the transit authority figured out how to clean paint and marker ink off of trains, artists sought new way to emboss their names and images. A bit of sandpaper only costs a few cents, but when scraped across glass or metal it transforms into a drawing implement that cannot be erased the way spray paint can.

At times, innovations in hip-hop culture have been sparked by tensions with laws and law enforcement. Alongside technical ability and creativity, a disregard for rules—whether on political grounds, out of necessity, out of a sense of rebellion, or out of a sense of exceptionalism—can be seen as an essential ingredient of hip-hop innovation. In some instances this has meant hip-hop heads engaging in acts that are considered illegal. Operating outside the law has come at a cost to some artists, as well as to some of those who follow in their footsteps, and others in their communities.

While *scratch tags* are an example of an illegal innovation, hip-hop artists often come up with creative solutions to regulation and repression that do not involve breaking any laws. Hip-hop DJs and producers began by using available resources, such as old records, in inventive ways to create a new style of music. But when the legal system came down on them for using pieces of other artists' music, producers responded by sampling shorter clips and distorting them, hunting down records that were not copyrighted, and using more sounds and instrumentation that they created on their own.

Whether it is metaphorical dances between artists and the legal system or the literal dances of b-boys and b-girls who lay discarded cardboard on the sidewalk to create dance floors, these types of invention do not occur *in spite of* restrictive circumstances, they occur *because* of them.[10]

"Can you teach people to be more creative?" someone once asked the philosopher Nelson Goodman. "Yes," he answered. When asked how, he replied, "Give them harder problems." Faced with racism, classism, ageism, and other forms of structural subjugation, many young people have developed the courage to break rules, the audacity to believe they can do things that have never been done, and the creativity to imagine how. This is hip-hop.

Hip-hop's music, culture, and creative resourcefulness originated in low-income, urban, predominantly black and Latino communities in the United States. While its roots extend around the world, particularly throughout the African diaspora, the sensibility, style, and spirit of hip-hop culture could only have brewed on this country's concrete.[11]

And yet hip-hop was never exclusively an urban thing, a low-income thing, a black thing, or a United States thing. Since its inception, hip-hop has touched and been touched by people from broader communities. In a matter of years, what started as a splash rippling through neighborhoods of New York City grew into tsunami-size waves rushing over continents, flowing into the biggest venues and markets in the world, and lapping up against individuals' psyches and souls.

Hip-hop is not the first cultural movement to emerge out of oppressive social conditions in the United States and rise to international popularity. Nor is it the first to combine music, dance, visual arts, and an overall aesthetic. The blues, jazz, early R&B, and funk all preceded hip-hop as art forms that emanated out of African American communities enduring the particular blend of racism and economic inequalities endemic to this country's history. Each of these musical genres was accompanied by specific styles of dance, dress, and speech—a culture. Pulling energy and influence from all of these predecessors, hip-hop has become a lasting means of understanding, existing in, and shaping the surrounding world.

A clear manifestation of this is the way in which rappers and hip-hop producers have taken their ability to lyrically and musically flip things into the business arena. Musicians from other genres have used their creativity to go from situations of extremely limited resources to tremendous wealth, but generally their creativity has been their product. They have sold their songs through preexisting systems of commerce, with businessmen—who were often white—reaping the lion's share of the profits.

In some instances, these musicians have also promoted other products, but they generally appeared as hired spokespeople, not business owners. Hip-hop artists have not just created a new kind of music; they have integrated how music is made and linked with other commodities, and altered systems of ownership and distribution in ways not previously considered possible by artists of any race.

Like all art forms that achieve popularity in this capitalist economy, hip-hop music has been co-opted and commodified by wealthy white outsiders to the culture. However, unlike any antecedents, hip-hop artists have refused to limit their creativity and swagger to their cultural products. By starting and cross-promoting their own record labels, media companies, clothing brands, lines of fragrances, and beverage companies, hip-hop stars have seamlessly enmeshed a fresh approach to the art of business into the business of art.

Hip-hop was forged in resistance to oppression, but hip-hop artists have demonstrated that the culture is no longer synonymous with struggle. Goodman may be right that "harder problems" breed creativity, but hip-hop's financial success has shown that such problems do not need to have life-or-death consequences for those involved; they can be theoretical, conceptual, strategic.

"Does the edge exist because you're poor, or does the edge exist because you're willing to challenge your reality in ways others may not?" asks hip-hop artist and activist Rha Goddess.[12] She cautions against falling into a paradigm in which struggling and starving are romanticized as prerequisites for creativity. The racism, classism, and ageism that inspired the birth of hip-hop still exist and continue to instigate innovations, but hip-hop cannot and should not be defined by desperation.

Ten years ago, if you asked a class full of fourteen-year-olds what they wanted to be when they grew up, a handful would have responded, "a rapper." Ask the question of current ninth-graders and several of those students will respond, "rapper-entrepreneurs." This melding of hip-hop art, identity, and industry led a man who grew up in the housing projects of Marcy to have clothing products at Macy's. Flipping his skills as an emcee to build his own entertainment/lifestyle conglomerate, Brooklyn-born Jay-Z returned to the mic in 2005, a year after becoming president and CEO of Def Jam Recordings, to spell it out for anyone who didn't understand: "I'm not a businessman, *I'm a business*, maaan!"[13]

Although the multibillion-dollar industries that hip-hop has spawned are some of the most visible manifestations of the power and potential of hip-hop, the spirit of hip-hop is not at all limited to the realm of business. Hip-hop does not just concern itself with the content of music, culture, and commerce; its infectious mind-set and irreverent swagger rush into all aspects of society—from graphic design to community organizing to culinary arts. Hip-hop may have begun as a result of young people with limited resources figuring out how to find a power source so they could throw a party, but the same sensibilities have led to building the power of political parties.

Some hip-hop icons have built organizations and movements directed toward electoral engagement. Russell Simmons founded and serves as chair of the board of the Hip Hop Summit Action Network, a nonprofit organization that does a variety of community engagement and youth development work, including voter education and registration. Leading up to the 2004 elections, Sean "Diddy" Combs founded Citizen Change, a political service group that enlisted celebrities such as Mary J. Blige, Leonardo DiCaprio, and 50 Cent to encourage voting among the hip-hop generation. It's difficult to determine the precise effect of Diddy's "Vote or Die!" campaign, but 2004 saw the largest turnout of young voters in over thirty years.[14]

Jim Jones, Capone-N-Noreaga, the Beastie Boys, and many other hip-hop celebrities joined Simmons and Diddy to speak out against New York's Rockefeller drug laws. By drawing tens of thousands of people to rallies and releasing viral online videos, these artists brought much-needed public attention to the organizing efforts that drug policy reform and prison reform activists had been engaged in for decades against the mandatory sentencing laws. In 2009, after thirty-six years, the Rockefeller drug laws were overhauled to remove their most draconian elements.

Other groups like the Hip Hop Caucus and the League of Young Voters bring innovative organizing tactics to work with the hip-hop generation. Over the past six years, the Hip Hop Caucus has blended hip-hop culture, media, and grassroots organizing to build a 700,000-person membership base and launch national campaigns from "Green the Block" to the "Respect My Vote!" national bus tour.[15]

The League of Young Voters—which was initiated with the name "League of Hip Hop Voters"—has created a year-round, multipronged approach to voter organizing and education.[16] League chapters across the country register voters, put out voter guides to provide young voters with accessible information on all the candidates, and work to keep pressure on politicians once they are elected.

Hip-hop heads infuse the culture and sensibilities into their lives and work, no matter what they do. As a chef, author, and food-justice activist, Bryant Terry merges politics, culinary arts, and hip-hop. The section titles of his cookbook, *Vegan Soul Kitchen*, make reference to Kanye West, Outkast, and Method Man lyrics and each recipe is accompanied by a soundtrack. Leading up to the release of the book, Bryant borrowed a move from contemporary emcees. Like rappers releasing mixtapes to build hype for coming albums, Terry released free recipes over the Internet.

His publisher was concerned he was saturating the market with his material and that potential customers might not feel the need to buy the book when it came out. Terry, who had recently seen Lil Wayne's album *The Carter III* debut at number one on the charts after Wayne had flooded the streets and Internet with mixtapes, held his ground and his book is now the top-selling soul food cookbook and within the top twenty vegan cookbooks on the popular online book retailer Amazon.com.[17]

The above examples involve bringing fresh approaches to entrenched arenas. Multiple definitions of the word "fresh" apply here—*fresh* in the conventional sense of the word, meaning newly made or obtained, but also hip-hop *fresh*, which fits somewhere between "dope" and "hot" in the long list of words that hip-hop heads use to describe something favorably. And, of course, in Bryant Terry's instance, fresh has a third meaning, referring to the ingredients with which he is encouraging people to cook! What is most significant though, what makes each of these endeavors *hip-hop* beyond overt references to the culture, is the way in which their architects have pioneered new approaches to old fields.

To some, then, "Hip Hop Genius"—the phrase that Ewell, Ellis, Simmons, Green, Wilkins, and I came up with during our 2005 meeting to describe the creative resourcefulness intrinsic to hip-hop—may sound redundant.[18] If the term "hip-hop" in and of itself implies such brilliance, why even add the word "genius"?

The English word "genius" was derived from the Latin root "gignere," meaning "to produce." It also had early ties to the Arabic word "jinn," which was used to describe individual spirits with supernatural powers. Prior to the late eighteenth century, *genius* was used to describe the magical force of an individual or a nation. In the decades leading up to the nineteenth century, European scholars began shifting the meaning of the word, using it to convey "the godlike power of invention, of creation, of making what never was before," which they used to describe the brilliant works of artists such as Homer and Michelangelo.[19]

Explaining why physicist Richard Feynman was considered the genius of his generation, biographer James Gleick concludes, "Those who tried to take Feynman's measure always came back to originality. . . . The generation coming up behind him, with the advantage of hindsight, still found nothing predictable in the paths of his thinking. He seemed perversely and dangerously bent on disregarding standard methods."[20]

This explanation suggests that anything dubbed *genius* must be innovative not only in its results but also in its approach. It implies that a paradigm shift has occurred; someone has flipped or altered a deep-seated understanding of how things work.

More recently, in introducing *Black Genius: African American Solutions to African American Problems*, one of the volume's editors, Walter Mosley, returned to the early notion of *genius* as something that characterizes a populace. "We understand genius to be that quality which crystallizes the hopes and talents and character of a people," Mosley writes. "This kind of genius is something we all share. It is a presence where absence once reigned. It is the possibility for a people to look into their hearts and to see a life worth living."[21]

From supernatural abilities to collective solutions, from disregarding standard methods to the power of invention, the word *genius* carries multiple connotations. All of these meanings are relevant to the concept of Hip Hop Genius.

Given that people have diverse, expansive, and conflicting perspectives of hip-hop, the addition of the word *genius* focuses attention on its majestic, creative, resourceful spirit. For people who view hip-hop as nothing more than a celebration of violence, sexism, homophobia, curse words, and a flagrant disregard for grammatical rules, just looking at these two phrases in conjunction with one another is a healthy exercise. Hip Hop . . . Genius . . . Hip Hop. Genius. HipHopGenius.

Young people who feel connected to hip-hop culture and are being slept on by society can benefit from considering the phrase *Hip Hop Genius*. The greater the potential for their culture and actions to be accorded respect, the more self-confidence and hope can flourish.

Researchers have found that when students of color are asked to indicate their race at the beginning of a standardized test, on average they receive lower scores than control groups who are given the same test without being asked to identify their race. Social psychologists believe this stems out of a fear that their race is or may be perceived to be a disadvantage; they refer to this phenomenon as "stereotype threat."[22] In direct contrast then, the concept of Hip Hop Genius has the potential to create *stereotype promise*.

Given that hip-hop is commonly associated with young people of color in urban environments, and given that this population has been perpetually portrayed by media outlets as "superpredators,"[23] the concept of Hip Hop Genius serves to challenge the typecasting of boys and girls in the 'hood.[24] By subverting the preconceptions of people who view inner-city children of color as criminals and charity cases, the possibility of those people acting as allies across race and class lines increases.

For those interested in dismantling systems of oppression and building a more just society, Hip Hop Genius is an essential ingredient. As Brazilian educator Paolo Freire writes, "The oppressed can overcome the contradiction in which they are caught only when this perception enlists them in the struggle to free themselves."[25] The more intentional everyone is in honoring and cultivating young peoples' creativity and sense of empowerment, the more profound the changes young people will be able to enact both to their personal circumstances and to biased social structures.

Hip Hop Genius holds the potential to play an important role in seeking solutions to global challenges. Our planet, as a whole, is facing a variety of situations defined by limited resources—most notably, the impending global energy crisis.

Wealthy people, companies, and countries all possess money and access to state-of-the-art equipment, but they have not necessarily cultivated the sensibilities needed to be resourceful. Identifying and honoring a form of genius that is sometimes noticed, but commonly ignored, trivialized, co-opted, and commodified, lends this raw brilliance the traction, recognition, and respect needed for it to spread like *Wild Style*.[26]

Discovery, development, and original thought are at the core of Hip Hop Genius. This focus on artistic, intellectual, and technical innovation makes education a natural starting point when considering how to foster and support this brand of brilliance. Learning and teaching are *fundamental* to the well-being and growth of young people and our society, yet our education system abysmally fails so many.

As the statistics and stories in chapter 4 of this book demonstrate, this failure has been most egregious when it comes to the exact demographic of young people who have been at the forefront of hip-hop's creation and evolution. This is a powerful indication of the impact that the Hip Hop Genius meme could have on the education system.

Much of hip-hop education thus far has been thought about within the context of classrooms in fairly conventional schools and out-of-school programs. Most often hip-hop is seen as a set of materials and skills that can replace the content of previous lesson plans. Instead of studying the novels of Joseph Conrad, classes study the lyrics of Joe

Budden; instead of learning to write sonnets and haikus, they learn to write sixteens and hooks.

Embodying Hip Hop Genius in an educational setting is deeper and more complex than bringing a rap song into an English class, painting a graffiti mural in a hallway, or inviting a breakdance troupe to a school assembly. It involves rethinking the very ways in which learning occurs. This is what the phrase "hip-hop pedagogy" should mean: an approach to teaching and learning that is specific to hip-hop.

But while "hip-hop pedagogy" has become an increasingly popular term in the last few years, little has been written about what might constitute the unique qualities of a hip-hop style of teaching and learning. The number of school principals who are members of the hip-hop generation is rapidly increasing, yet there has been little public dialogue about hip-hop leadership traits or the possibilities of hip-hop schools.

In many large cities, fewer than half of the black males who enter ninth grade graduate four years later. How might things change for these young men and others if schools could truly personify the spirit of Hip Hop Genius, breaking with conventions to provide something fresh, functional, and fly? What would it look like to transform the education industrial complex in the same kinds of ways that hip hoppers have freaked the music industry?

This book exists to bust open these conversations.

Chapter 1 introduces an innovative school, the High School for Recording Arts. Throughout its twelve years of operation in St. Paul, Minnesota, the school has avoided the limitations of traditional educational practices by blending elements of a variety of alternative educational techniques with original flavor. Through inventive and sometimes unusual approaches, the school has found unique ways to honor the brilliance of young people who have been ignored, shunned, and feared by the institutions charged with educating them. By giving readers a tour through the halls of the school and a description of the pedagogy, curriculum, and philosophy employed by the school, this chapter suggests a set of creative and promising educational practices that could be reproduced and remixed in other schools or used as inspiration for innovation in other sectors.

Because HSRA is so different from traditional schools, it can be hard to picture how the pedagogy, curriculum, and philosophy play out on a day-to-day basis. Chapter 2 follows a student through one full school day, demonstrating how the ideas described in the previous chapter manifest in the daily reality of a school community. Though it is only a description of *one* day of *one* student's experience, this chapter tethers theory to practice and provides a snapshot of how the school's philosophies, values, and methodologies affect individual students.

To understand HSRA, you have to understand how it came to exist. Chapter 3 shares stories of the school's creation and evolution by offering an intimate introduction to its founder, David "TC" Ellis. Tying stories from TC's childhood and his experiences recording with superstars such as Prince and George Clinton to challenges he has faced running the school, chapter 3 teases out unconventional yet essential qualities of TC's leadership style. From repurposing gangsta rappers' recording equipment to working with gang leaders to help squash beefs at the school, TC's trajectory holds tangible examples of the bold, unorthodox actions that exemplify Hip Hop Genius. Without proposing that anyone should or could follow directly in TC's footsteps, these stories can provoke readers, both in and outside the field of education, to reconsider what is possible and to hustle hard.

Describing problems that plague public education in this country, chapter 4 contextualizes the struggles and successes of HSRA's students and the school itself. By presenting obstacles that HSRA has encountered in the past few years, this chapter introduces common challenges that inevitably have an impact on educators attempting to create schools that effectively serve low- and no-income students of color.

Such challenges can be especially harsh for educators who incorporate hip-hop into their practice. Yet the field of hip-hop education is growing. Chapter 5 surveys the current hip-hop education landscape, identifying how HSRA fits into several trends in the field and proposing Hip Hop Genius as a new iteration of hip-hop education that is more radical in its approach and better positioned to fully honor the creativity and ingenuity of urban young people.

Chapter 6 suggests specific strategic possibilities for spreading the school's work and the ethos of Hip Hop Genius. From replicating the school's design in new sites to turning the program in Minnesota into an open source laboratory for other educators and hip-hop heads to visit and learn from, this chapter explores how HSRA can be most effective in influencing ideas and infusing inspiration into the hip-hop and education communities.

There is so much potential for beauty and creation, and yet violence and destruction dominate headlines and minds. Children—full of energy and ideas—are neglected, punished because of how much melanin they have in their skin and how little money they have in their pockets. Personal greed, contempt, and contentment too often triumph over asking hard questions, striving for equality, and making meaningful change.

Society has been sleeping for too long. It's time to back-flip on that mattress.

## NOTES

1. Christopher B. Swanson and Amy M. Hightower, "Diplomas Count 2008: School to College" PowerPoint slide 4, http://www.edweek.org/media/ew/dc/2008/DC08_Presentation_FINAL.pdf (accessed December 16, 2010).

2. Further statistics on the demographics of students who are not graduating from high school are provided in chapter 4.

3. John Jennings, "Dezyne Klass: Exploring Image-Making through the Visual Culture of Hip Hop," in Design Studies: Theory and Research in Graphic Design, ed. Audrey Bennett. (New York: Princeton Architectural Press, 2006), 241.

4. Jennings, "Dezyne Klass," 242.

5. Wasalu Muhammad Jaco aka Lupe Fiasco, "Just Might Be Okay," Lupe Fiasco's Food & Liquor, 1st and 15th/Atlantic, 2005, compact disc.

6. I have chosen to use the term "breakdancing" rather than "b-boying," which is considered by many the more authentic term for hip-hop dance. This decision was made because the inclusion of the word "dance" clarifies what I am referring to and because it does not carry the same gender privileging that "b-boying" implies.

7. Robert A. Caro, The Power Broker: Robert Moses and the Fall of New York (New York: Knopf, 1974).

8. Jeff Chang, Can't Stop Won't Stop: A History of the Hip-Hop Generation (New York: Picador, 2005), 13.

9. Chang, Can't Stop Won't Stop, 118.

10. B-boys and b-girls are hip-hop dancers.

11. For a more comprehensive explanation of hip-hop as black American music, see Imani Perry, Prophets of the Hood: Politics and Poetics in Hip Hop (Durham, N.C.: Duke University Press, 2004).

12. Rha Goddess, "Scarcity and Exploitation: The Myth and Reality of the Struggling Hip-Hop Artist," in *Total Chaos: The Art and Aesthetics of Hip-Hop*, ed. Jeff Chang (New York: Basic Civitas, 2006), 346.

13. Shawn C. Carter aka Jay-Z, "Diamonds from Sierra Leone Remix," on *Late Registration*, by Kanye West, Roc-A-Fella/Island Def Jam, 2005, compact disc.

14. Jose Antonio Vargas, "Vote or Die? Well, They Did Vote," *Washington Post*, November 9, 2004, http://www.washingtonpost.com/wp-dyn/articles/ A35290–2004Nov8.html (accessed June 12, 2010).

15. For more information about the Hip Hop Caucus, see http://www .hiphopcaucus.org/ (accessed December 16, 2010).

16. The League of Young Voters has also been known as the League of Pissed-Off Voters. For more information, see http://www.theleague.com (accessed December 16, 2010).

17. Amazon.com, http://www.amazon.com/Vegan-Soul-Kitchen-Bryant -Terry/dp/0738212288 (accessed June 18, 2010).

18. The term "hip-hop" can be spelled several different ways, with and without hyphen or space and with varying capitalization. Throughout this book it will be spelled, "hip-hop" with the exception of when it appears in direct quotes, titles, and in the phrase "Hip Hop Genius."

19. James Gleick, *Genius: The Life and Science of Richard Feynman* (New York: Pantheon Books, 1992), 313.

20. Gleick, *Genius*, 323.

21. Walter Mosley, introduction, *Black Genius: African American Solutions to African American Problems*, ed. Walter Mosley et al. (New York: W. W. Norton, 1999), 12.

22. Claude M. Steele and Joshua Aronson, "Stereotype Threat and the Test Performance of Academically Successful African Americans," in *The Black-White Test Score Gap*, ed. Christopher Jencks and Meredith Phillips (Washington, D.C.: Brookings Institution Press, 1998), 401.

23. Elaine Brown, *The Condemnation of Little B* (Boston: Beacon Press, 2002), 108–11.

24. This refers to the title of John Singleton's 1991 film portraying urban youth in south central Los Angeles.

25. Paulo Freire, *Pedagogy of the Oppressed* (New York: Herder and Herder, 1971), 34.

26. This refers to the title of Charlie Ahearn's 1983 film depicting early hip-hop legends engaging in hip-hop arts. It is considered by many to be the first hip-hop motion picture.

## (1)

# HIP HOP HIGH

Be a true friend to him
Before the shit put an end to him
Give a pen to him
Or lock him in a studio with a mic
'cause on the reals
It might save his life.

—The Roots

Do not train a child to learn by force or harshness; but direct them
to it by what amuses their minds, so that you may be better able to
discover with accuracy the peculiar bent of the genius of each.

—Plato

Our goal is to get students mad enough to want more and smart
enough to get it in a whole different way.

—Tony Simmons

The first thing you see as you enter the High School for Recording
Arts (HSRA) is a professional-quality recording studio with a red "In
Session" light over the door. It's immediately clear that this studio is

official: huge mixing boards, large flat-screen monitors, a glass window that reveals a microphone booth, waves of black foam on the walls, and the requisite leather sofa in the corner.

Donte Suttle, aka "Humble Child," and "Lil Layne" Bellamy are debating which combination of microphone and software is best for creating the Auto-Tune vocoder effect that T-Pain's spate of R&B hits recently brought back from obscurity.[1] Donte is seated in an ergonomic chair in front of a keyboard. He's wearing a black fitted cap and a long black T-shirt. Lil Layne is seated across from him, wearing a wave cap and baggy sweatpants. Donte and Lil Layne are studio engineers, and both of these men are graduates of the school.

The studio director, "Uncle Phil" Winden, enters and is asked his opinion on the matter. Phil is in his forties. His closely cropped hair and beard include some gray hairs and his clothes fit a bit tighter than his younger associates. A quick conversation with Uncle Phil makes two things clear: one, he has a lot of experience as a professional studio engineer; and two, he is excited to teach others how to use all the fancy equipment at their fingertips.

A stroll around the school shows that beyond the recording studios this place has some obvious differences from Central, Highland Park, Como, and the other big high schools in the Twin Cities. First of all, there are no classrooms! There is a giant open workspace, approximately five thousand square feet divided into distinct work areas by low corrugated steel partitions, lined with counters holding computers.

In one of the five work areas, a group of twelve students is sitting in a circle of chairs discussing the book *Monster* by Walter Dean Myers. In another work area, seven students are seated at computers working quietly. There is one Latina student and one white young man. All the other students in both these groups are black.

A young woman with her hood pulled over her head has a stack of pamphlets on teen health and sexually transmitted diseases on one side of her computer and a book on website design on the other. Next to her, a young man wearing headphones is using spreadsheet software to create a rubric for how to rate emcees. Behind these two, another student is turned away from her computer, discussing her idea for a research project on the history of the WNBA with a woman in her thirties who's wearing a USB jump drive on a lanyard around her neck.

At the other end of the giant room, there is an open space that can be separated from the work areas by sliding glass garage doors. This area, which is referred to as "the blacktop," has a stage in the front and a DJ booth with a soundboard and spotlight in the back. In the middle of the space there are cafeteria tables. Six students sit on top of tables, their feet on the attached benches. They are talking and laughing. Two of them have their cell phones out and, during lulls in the conversation, they return to texting.

One sidewall of the area is covered in graffiti; students' nicknames and tags, a cartoon keyboard and musical notes, and a big "Studio 4" piece are spray-painted across the wall. Along the other side of the room, there are vending machines—one of which offers blank CDs for a dollar a piece.

In the hallways that extend off of the large room, photos line the walls, telling visual stories of students and staff traveling the world together— Africa, Guatemala, New York, Washington, D.C., and other cities across the United States. Additional photos feature an impressive list of African American celebrities visiting the school—scholar Michael Eric Dyson, actress Lynn Whitfield, jazz trombonist Delfeayo Marsalis, and rappers such as Ice Cube, Juelz Santana, and Chris "Kazi" Rolle.

Doors along each hall open onto smaller rooms containing administrative offices; multimedia workspaces; a dance studio complete with wood floors, mirrored walls, and a ballet barre; a graphic design lab; and a record label boardroom. The boardroom is decorated with clocks that show the time in major cities, a large whiteboard, and color posters of the label's album releases. One of the posters features a rap album by David "TC" Ellis, the founder of the school. Another poster advertises the release of an album by an alumnus and current employee of the school, Codie Wilson aka "Monsta Codie Indiana."

Down the hall from the boardroom, TC is standing talking to two students. He appears to be almost twenty years older than the image on the poster and he has traded in the sunglasses he was rocking in the photo for a baggy rugby shirt and a gold chain with a medallion in the shape of the African continent. Leaning up against the wall, flipping his cell phone open and shut against his leg, he is breaking down to the two young men some of the ways in which he sees students hold each other back from achieving greatness.

Without knowing anything specific about the curriculum or population, one thing is clear just from wandering the halls: HSRA is not your
typical high school.

## HYBRID FLAVOR

Hip-hop has never been about creating fly things from scratch. Of
course, there is an irony to this statement because early hip-hop disc
jockeys created so much fly music from the *scratching* of records. But
the records they were scratching contained musical compositions by
other artists who came before them.

DJs began selecting and repeating the most climactic segments of
other musicians' recordings as part of live routines they would perform to
keep partygoers dancing. The practice evolved into a set of compositional
techniques that now create the backbone of the majority of hip-hop
songs. By merging multiple looped samples and original instrumentation,
audial pastiches are created that, in one song, can fuse musical gems
from multiple genres that may have never previously intermingled.

This sort of creative collaging has long been celebrated as a quality of
geniuses. In his 1767 *Essay on Original Genius*, William Duff discusses
the genius's imagination as "the mind not only reflect[ing] on its own
operations" but also as a faculty by which one "assembles the various
ideas . . . treasured up in the repository of the memory, compounding or
disjoining them at pleasure; and which, by its plastic power of inventing
new associations of ideas, and of combining them with infinite variety,
is enabled to present a creation of its own."[2]

In the painstaking process of combining disparate components to
craft an original composition, every decision must be deliberate. Finding clips that sound good on their own may take DJs hours of digging,
but the bigger challenge is that the samples have to syncopate and sound
even better together. As more layers are added, the difficulty of align-
ing pieces in a harmonious manner increases. Not only must producers
balance these challenges but, in order to be successful, they must do it
in such a way that establishes their own trademark style.

In his essay on the aesthetics of hip-hop literature, Adam Mansbach
refers to hip-hop's instinct to borrow and blend as "intellectual democ-

racy through collage."[3] This cut-and-paste intellectual democracy is exemplified in the DJing of Afrika Bambaataa, who would mix Grand Funk Railroad with the Monkees and drop a Malcolm X speech on top.[4] No matter how corny the Monkees' reputation was, if they had a dope drum break, it was getting played. The rule, as Mansbach points out, is that "whatever's hot is worthy of adoption, regardless of its location or context."[5]

This tradition of sampling and reassembling is not integral just to hip-hop music but to other aspects of the culture as well, for instance, dance. As Nelson George points out: "What came to be labeled [breakdancing], was actually a medley of moves adapting a number of sources—the shuffling, sliding steps of James Brown; the dynamic, platformed dancers on Don Cornelius's syndicated *Soul Train* television show; Michael Jackson's robotic moves that accompanied the 1974 hit 'Dancin' Machine'; the athletic leg whips and spins of kung fu movies all of which were funneled through the imagination of black New Yorkers."[6] Capoiera moves and Latin dance steps could be added to this list, as well as other influences, large and small.

HSRA has taken this approach and implemented it in the field of education. The founders of the school do not claim to have invented the educational and youth development practices at play within the school. Rather, they are proud of the ways in which they have sampled, mixed, screwed, and chopped a medley of innovative approaches to education, entrepreneurship, artistic production, youth development, and the provision of support services.

HSRA's hybrid flavor comes from blending elements from a vast array of sources, most notably from a several-decade-long lineage of public alternative schools that have carved out niches for themselves through negotiating local politics, using limited funds effectively, and extreme dedication from their staff members, students, families, and communities. These schools have challenged conventional hierarchical power structures as well as commonly accepted delivery methods and mandated curricula.

By engaging students as leaders and scholars, running classes democratically, introducing a wide variety of materials, building a supportive culture, and offering students opportunities to learn in real-world contexts, many of these alternative programs have managed to attract and retain students, helping them to get excited about learning, earn diplomas, and prepare for life beyond high school.

If HSRA were an album, there would be extensive liner notes attributing the influences to which the school owes aspects of its unique composition. Inevitably, as there are so many elements from so many sources, some much-deserved head nods would be missed along the way, but what is crucial to understand is that there are many trajectories from which these educational solutions emerge; the genius of HSRA is the fusion.

## RESPECT'S THE GAME

To explain what makes HSRA an extraordinary school, multiple concepts must be unpacked—project-based learning, advisories, authentic assessment, youth empowerment—but there is one fundamental value from which all decisions about how to run the school stem, that all students feel when they enter the school, and that troubles the traditional-minded: *The respect for the brilliance and resilience of young people— especially kids from the 'hood.* Students are not seen as problems to be solved or empty vessels waiting to be filled. They are valued as thinkers, artists, and entrepreneurs—survivors and thrivers.

There is a technical term for this value that is used in the nonprofit community: Asset-Based Community Development. This concept came about as a response to the most common way that institutions in this country treat communities of color with limited economic resources—a dehumanizing, "needs-based" presumption of deficiencies.

An increasing number of institutions are recognizing that the deficit model is the wrong approach. Some make efforts to embrace young peoples' skills and capacities but are too stuck in their old ways to move much beyond lip service. However, in the past fifteen years, the most progressive schools and youth programs have focused enormous energy on finding solutions in the strengths and talents within their communities. This trend permeates HSRA.

By requiring students to take the lead in designing their own curriculum, HSRA honors students' individual identities and capabilities. By partnering with social service agencies to provide support services,

HSRA shows respect for students' fundamental rights to physical safety, health, housing, and transportation. And by creating real-world leadership opportunities, HSRA shows students the highest form of respect, the expectation that they can and should be traveling the world, representing their community, and making a difference in the lives of others.

## ANOTHER LEVEL OF LEADERSHIP FOR STUDENTS

One of the strongest manifestations of the respect that students are afforded can be seen through the student-run record label and event production company, Another Level Entertainment. Through the label, students are empowered to make decisions typically assumed to be the domain of adults.

"I'm in the middle of everything," explains Buki, an HSRA senior, who is the current president of Another Level Entertainment. Before coming to HSRA, Buki attended Central High School for one semester. She didn't feel she was getting anything out of her time there and she intentionally got kicked out so that she could transfer to HSRA.

When she first arrived at HSRA, Buki wanted to be a rapper. She recalls that "after about a year and a half pursuing that dream, I realized that rapping wasn't quite my swagg." Instead, Buki discovered her passion for "helping other people handle their business."

When she's not attending courses at the local community college or working on the nonprofit she recently founded, Buki now spends much of her time making phone calls to arrange performances, facilitating meetings, and coordinating the production of an album promoting nonviolence, which is being put together by the school's Urban Music workshop.

Throughout the label's history, the students who staff Another Level Entertainment have focused on a diverse array of projects. Over the years they have collaborated with adults at the school to produce peers' albums, fulfill recording and performance contracts with businesses and government agencies who hire them to raise awareness about topics such as seatbelt safety and the importance of staying in school, manage the label's finances, arrange performances, host school events, and produce a weekly radio show, the Fo-Show, on the local commercial hip-hop station.[7]

This is a unique approach to running a high school and a unique approach to running a record label. But it is especially distinctive given the cultural context of the geographic area in which the school is located. The school's education director, Paula Anderson, explains that the school "is one of the few places in Minnesota where African American culture is dominant."

The school's predominantly black student body has grown up surrounded by a predominantly white culture. Prior to attending HSRA, many students have been in schools that have little in common with their home cultures and experiences outside of school.

It can be eye-opening for students to be exposed to materials from outside their cultural contexts, but when the language, style, and subject matter they encounter in classes and other school activities is consistently foreign to them, students can become alienated. This has an adverse effect on achievement.[8]

In order to better serve students, educators must address this "cultural mismatch."[9] The multicultural tapestry of this country's current student population is incredibly complex. Bridging cultural divides is not, literally or figuratively, a black and white issue. Nor is it simply a matter of celebrating the food or customs of the many cultures from which students come. A deeper integration of young peoples' cultural experiences is needed in order for schools to be relevant to their students.

There are many ways that schools can and should engage students' cultural identities more thoroughly. Due to hip-hop's pervasive nature and the fact that it is such a wellspring of cultural cues, vocabulary, and other forms of identification, it holds great power as a source of cultural connections. Through celebrating and engaging with hip-hop, HSRA honors what is, for many students, their deepest passion.

It is extremely important to acknowledge that by no means do all young people—black, Latino, or otherwise—identify with hip-hop culture. For instance, HSRA has had students who prefer rock music and goth style. Nevertheless, hip-hop is one of HSRA students' primary cultural contexts and by incorporating a hip-hop record label into the program, HSRA sends the message, even to students who don't personally identify with hip-hop, that a spectrum of cultural and "countercultural" experiences is being recognized and engaged in the school community.

The fact that students are entrusted to run the record label, that they have access to professional quality equipment, and that this work is not relegated to one of the common diminutive categories of "after-school project" or "elective" but rather is viewed as a central piece of their academic program communicates a high prioritization of young peoples' interests and capabilities—even to students not personally passionate about hip-hop and not directly involved in Another Level Entertainment.

## STUDENT VOICES ARE HEARD

HSRA's embrace of students' participation in hip-hop music and culture goes beyond the student-run record label. The school's logo has a picture of a kid in front of a microphone. His hat is turned back and he's wearing headphones.[10] Students who have consistent attendance and are in good academic standing earn an "All Access Pass," which allows them to spend free time, afternoons, weekends, and evenings in the recording studios.

Every week, students are not only allowed but encouraged to perform in a schoolwide showcase, which is called a Pick Me Up.[11] In the context of school, a young person can don sunglasses and a fitted hat, grab a microphone, and spit lyrics straight from the heart, dancing across a stage followed by a spotlight, while being cheered on by fellow students and staff.

This literal and figurative spotlight plays an important role in students' lives. For a host of reasons—including racism, classism, sexism, ageism, and homophobia—many students at HSRA have been ignored or told countless times, implicitly and explicitly, that their lives do not matter.

Some young people shut down as a result of such identity abuse. Others decide they will be seen and heard *one way or another*. For some, this means tireless investment in academic, athletic, entrepreneurial, or political pursuits. For others, it means acquiring luxury cars, flossy jewelry, and other accessories that will attract attention, by any means necessary. And for others, it means finding their way to the front page of the newspaper, even if it's for engaging in an act of violence or destruction. By offering opportunities to produce radio shows, CDs, and performance showcases, HSRA is providing students with creative and legal channels by which to be seen and heard.

HSRA also demonstrates respect for students by cultivating conditions that honor their lives and foster their success. For instance, like many other programs, HSRA has struggled with chronic absence and tardiness. In addition to coming up with consequences that discourage lateness, the staff and students have worked hard to understand the problem and generate innovative solutions.

One of the most fruitful changes they have instituted is to start later than almost any other high school in the country: The HSRA school day does not begin until 10 a.m. They came to this schedule shift organically through experience and dialogue, but scientific research, such as a study recently released in the *Journal of Clinical Sleep Medicine,* has since demonstrated that later school start times are actually more in line with teenagers' natural circadian rhythms. Despite the fact that data shows that later start times improve attendance and academic performance, few other schools have adjusted their schedules.[12]

The school day at HSRA also runs longer than most schools, officially ending at 4:30 p.m., with many students and staff members staying later to work on school projects, personal endeavors, and just to hang out. Given that most arrests of teenagers occur during weekday afternoons, keeping the school open during these times helps students stay productive and avoid dangerous situations.[13]

## STUDYING ISSUES RELEVANT TO STUDENTS' LIVES

How can students take adults seriously if those adults don't acknowledge the challenges students face during the eighteen hours every day that they are not in school? HSRA staff members design group projects and workshops that explore societal problems, such as homelessness and violence. Through these projects and workshops, students create products—often musical compilations—that present their research and ideas in ways that can inform and inspire deeper thinking and conversation among others.

Workshops on topics such as the prison–industrial complex address the race and class conflicts that students are experiencing but have rarely been invited to discuss or analyze in school settings. HSRA staff members and students identify dynamics of oppression that are playing out within the school community and build opportunities for group study and conversation.

When Libby Harris was in her first year as an advisor at the school, she was overwhelmed by the prevalence of homophobic and misogynistic language used by students. Sick of hearing students call each other "bitch" in the halls or use "gay" to describe something they didn't like, she decided to offer a workshop on "The Power of Words" to "examine the language of ethnic, gender, and sexual orientation bias."[14] Using materials from an organization called Teaching Tolerance, Libby crafted a curriculum for a workshop.

"In most schools, I couldn't do what I'm doing in this workshop," Libby reflected after the first week, "I couldn't give out a reading with words like 'bastard' and 'pussywhipped.'" Libby used this language to provoke students' thinking about the ways in which many words that insult men actually contain hidden insults to women. Initially her use of such language inspired some snickers and giggles, but eventually the group of students who had elected to be a part of the workshop settled into a mature discussion that touched on topics that many said they'd never discussed openly before.

When Libby says she would not have been able to lead a workshop like the Power of Words at most schools, she is speaking from experience. Prior to coming to HSRA, Libby taught at a middle school in suburban Wisconsin, which was under referendum requiring all teachers to implement the same curriculum. There was no room for doing anything different for students who had unique interests or needs. She had been reprimanded for talking with her students about global warming and suggesting it might be a cause for concern.

By contrast, at HSRA students and staff are encouraged to spend time learning about and analyzing current events. At the school's inception, the only textbook that teachers used was the daily newspaper. More recently, during the fall of 2008, as the country geared up for a historic presidential election, the entire school read President Barack Obama's *Dreams from My Father: A Story of Race and Inheritance* and discussed the book in the context of the election and the media's coverage of the candidates.

These types of workshops and activities build on the work of educators like Paulo Freire, encouraging students to peel back the many layers of their realities, ask critical questions, imagine the world they would like to live in, and consider ways in which they can take action to become the change they want to see.[15]

## ALTERNATIVE APPROACHES TO ACADEMICS

If it is the music that initially attracts students to HSRA and the respect they receive that compels them to stay, it is the academic program that opens up new possibilities for their scholastic success. The key to the academic component of the school is that it too honors students' interests and intelligence.

Students are not forced through a four-year pipeline with standardized boxes to check off along the way, and the staff's role is not to lecture or issue unilateral assignments but rather to work with each student to customize her or his academic experience to maximize learning. Staff members work with each student to develop an individualized course of study that builds on that individual student's background, taps into their passions, and meets their needs as far as graduation requirements and skills necessary to pursue further education and employment.

How does something like this fit into the structure of a school? It is not possible to truly honor students' diverse interests, learning styles, strengths, and challenges if a bell is ringing every forty-five minutes and teachers are seeing more than one hundred students every day. So how do you move all students along toward graduation if every student is following a different trajectory?

## FROM CARNEGIE UNITS TO MOVING UNITS

In most high schools, the only way students can graduate is by receiving course credits. The only way they can acquire these credits is by sitting in specific classes with specific titles, such as "U.S. History," for a pre-determined amount of time every day for nine months.

In education lingo, the standard amount of time a student must spend in a class in order to earn credit is called a Carnegie Unit, which consists of 120 hours. This system does not measure what a student knows or can do; instead, it simply counts how many minutes they spent in a classroom.

At HSRA, there are five ways that students can earn credit, all of which involve *demonstrating* what they can do as a result of what they have learned.

1. The most encouraged and popular path to earning credits is through designing and completing projects. Each project can be done as an individual or in a small group and culminates in the presentation of an original product. One common example of a student project is the recording of an album. A student can earn Language Arts credit by authoring lyrics and liner notes; Social Studies credits by selecting and researching topics for songs on the album; Science credits by studying the physics of sound waves; and Math credits by developing a budget that calculates production and reproduction costs. In this way, a student can develop core academic skills while fulfilling her dream to not only become a rapper but actually produce an album and get it into peoples' hands. Instead of sitting back and earning Carnegie units, students are moving units, earning money and respect.

2. Through workshops. These workshops may be led by school staff members, outside instructors, alumni, or fellow students. Some regularly offered workshops include Urban Music, through which students collectively produce an album about a social issue, such as HIV prevention; The Business of Music, which offers students an introduction to the commercial and legal issues related to the music industry; and Design, which gives students a chance to develop products for real-world clients.

3. Through daily blocks of time spent in their advisories focused on math, reading, and language arts. These group-study sessions were added to the school's design in recent years in response to pressure

from the Minnesota Department of Education to raise students' scores on high-stakes standardized tests. Some students and staff members feel that the daily chunks of time carved out for Concentrated Math, Quiet Reading, and Daily Language Arts are a hindrance to the individualized interest-based curriculum that lies at the heart of the academic program. Others appreciate the time set aside to ensure that all students are getting direct instruction in core academic subjects.

4. Through completing guided study packets that are structured to build skills and allow students to demonstrate their competency in specific academic areas. While advisors generally discourage students from trying to get lots of credits by completing packets, it can be an efficient way to "make up time" for students who are in their late teens or early twenties and feel the need to accelerate their journey to graduation.

5. Through Minnesota's Post-Secondary Education Option, which allows students to take college courses for free while in high school. Many states have similar programs, and increasing numbers of high school students are enrolling. Currently about fifteen HSRA students take advantage of this opportunity each year. Staff members are encouraging more students to consider this chance to get college credits and experience at no cost prior to graduation.

Through projects, workshops, academic blocks, packets, and college courses, students are expected to *show* what they know. Without a sophisticated system, it would be unfeasible for the staff of HSRA to keep track of the accomplishments of over two hundred students simultaneously engaged in their own unique blends of these methods. This would make it impossible to determine when students were qualified to graduate. To this end, HSRA has a list of "validations" that serve as the school's graduation requirements. On students' first day at the school, they are introduced to the validation system and empowered to take a lead role in keeping track of their own progress toward graduation.

Using a process pioneered by Dr. Wayne Jennings and colleagues at the St. Paul Open School, which TC attended in the late 1970s, HSRA has developed twelve "learning areas" and defined what students must produce in each area to demonstrate competence. These are the HSRA validations.

Some of HSRA's validations—such as Mathematics, Reading/Literary Analysis, and Science and Technology—are pulled directly from state standards, but they are put into language that is more accessible to students. Other validations—such as Artistic Expression and Appreciation, and Philosophical, Emotional, and/or Spiritual Awareness—emerged from school staff considering what they want all HSRA graduates to know and be able to do.

Most validations contain some state-mandated benchmarks and some school-determined criteria. For example, in the learning area of "Effective Communication," a student must pass the Minnesota Basic Standards Tests in Writing and Reading, but the student must also demonstrate "effective oral communication, which may include presentations, spoken word performances or recordings, interviews, participation in group discussions, formal oral responses, and effective day-to-day speaking."[16] In this way, HSRA blends samples of standardized assessment systems that may be used to measure students as they apply to colleges with a mix of skills that will be valuable for students in their future endeavors.

As students develop projects, select workshops, decide which guided study packets they would like to complete, and enroll in college courses, they communicate with their advisors about which validations each of these endeavors will help them achieve and how they will determine when the validations have been completed.

Advisors help students identify people who possess expertise in each learning area and can therefore serve as validators. For instance, for "Science and Technology," the validator must be a certified science instructor, while for a learning area like "Physical Education," the validator could be a boxing coach outside of the school who can verify that a student has demonstrated progress in that particular area.

The school has invested time and resources in developing *Project Excellence*, a proprietary software program designed to track each student's progress in demonstrating proficiency at the validations. Part of each student's responsibility is to document her or his progress in each learning area. Students are able to log into Project Excellence at school or from home to update their profile. Staff members can also access students' pages on Project Excellence to check on progress and correspond with students about their work.

## LINES OF DESIRE

When architects and urban planners design open outdoor spaces, sometimes they delay paving paths. Landscapers seed grass everywhere and then the designers sit back and wait.

Wherever the grass is worn down from frequent foot traffic, pavement is then laid. This process of letting pedestrians dictate the paths by walking where they want to go is referred to as "lines of desire."

The style of project-based learning at HSRA functions in a similar way. Rather than educators coming with a preconceived plan for what students will study, they seed possibilities everywhere and then hang back to see where students' interests draw them. Once students have tread their individual paths, the staff members figure out how to help solidify their course ways.

There are two key manners in which the HSRA educator's work differs from the designer's in the above metaphor. While the designer is looking for a general pattern among all walkers traversing their new green, HSRA staff must find a way to support each student on her or his own journey. Also, unlike pedestrians who all walk on concrete of the same density, grade, and texture, each learner needs customized reinforcements. In this way, educators also have to be alchemists, crafting a unique blend of elements to properly support each student.

Project-based learning is a pedagogical strategy that allows young people to determine their own paths. Out of the five ways for students to complete validations at HSRA, project-based learning is the furthest from traditional pedagogies. Yet it is an educational best practice that is currently used in schools around the world.

Organizations, such as Big Picture Learning, EdVisions, and High Tech High, have been demonstrating forms of project-based learning in their international, national, and state-based networks of schools and have all served as examples for HSRA. For over twenty-two years, the Buck Institute for Education has offered extensive resources on project-based learning; worked with school districts and networks, government agencies, universities, and foundations to increase the amount of learning conducted through projects; and studied the pedagogical style's efficacy.[17]

There is a spectrum of teaching strategies that can be referred to as "project-based." Some educators play a heavy role in the design and orchestration of projects. By selecting topics, articulating what steps must occur along the way, and requesting a specific outcome, the instructor guides a group of students through a project of the instructor's own design.

At the other end of the spectrum, educators invite students to generate individual projects that the students want to design and complete. This usually starts with a general area of interest—for example, a student might be fascinated by secret societies—or with an idea of a finished product a student wishes to create—such as a website about the illuminati. From there, educators work one-on-one with students to engage in "backward planning," determining what research will need to be done, skills practiced, materials collected, and relationships cultivated, in order to complete the project at hand.

HSRA focuses on individual and group projects driven by students' passions, because it guarantees that students' schoolwork will honor their talents and skills, and align with their interests and life goals. This keeps students engaged and increases their chances of reaching their goals. For example, an alumnus of HSRA, Young Menace, confesses: "I wasn't an angel, but when music was integrated, I was motivated."

While at HSRA, Young Menace watched the industry standard for music recording change from Digital Audio Tape (DAT) to ProTools. He learned how to use each system, as well as the importance of keeping up with the latest technology. As a high school student, Young Menace had self-produced albums circulating in the Twin Cities.

"No other school would've cared or even known," Young Menace reflects on his early production achievements. He now consults on music for the MTV, Discovery, and CW networks.

Young Menace's indictment of other schools is reinforced by the example of the George Westinghouse Career and Technical Education High School in Brooklyn, where Christopher George Latore Wallace, Trevor Tahiem Smith Jr., Kimberly Denise Jones, and Shawn Corey

Carter were all students within the same decade. Only Smith graduated. Despite a school that didn't recognize their potential, these four teenagers went on to become some of the biggest rap superstars ever: Notorious B.I.G., Busta Rhymes, Lil Kim, and Jay-Z. It is tragic, yet typical, that the school had no way to acknowledge and engage the brilliance of this cadre of young artists.

Student-generated projects ensure that young peoples' passions do not go ignored and unsupported. Whether a student is interested in hip-hop or hippopotami, project-based learning offers him the chance to explore his interests through designing and completing a project that has a purpose beyond checking off a school requirement. Because the content of their projects matter to them and because they are responsible for publicly presenting products that emerge out of their projects, students engaged in authentic project-based learning develop a level of expertise that is rare for high school students to possess.

Students at HSRA generate ideas, document their processes, and communicate with staff members by completing Project Proposal Forms for each project they initiate. The forms contain exercises to help them through the five stages of their project: Questioning, Research and Investigation, Progress Updates, Final Product and Presentation, and Reflection.

For instance, an HSRA senior, Reidun Saxerud, began with an interest in the popular Harry Potter book series by J. K. Rowling. In the Questioning stage of planning her project, Reidun used a thought-mapping diagram to turn this interest into a guiding question that she could develop a project to explore: "What makes the Harry Potter series good literature?" She also set goals for what she hoped to learn, what skills she hoped to develop, how she hoped the project would benefit others, and how she would assess herself upon completion.

In the Research and Investigation stage of her project, Reidun diagramed and summarized the resources such as books, websites, and people that she would draw upon to complete her project. Her resource list included all of the Harry Potter books that had been released, several websites that analyzed the series, and interviews and meetings with Paula Anderson, the school's education director, who is a certified English instructor.

In the Progress Updates stage, Reidun set target dates for each of the tasks she would need to complete. Her Project Steps began with "Learning literary terms," such as allegory and personification. Reidun wanted to be able to effectively analyze and argue the books' merits. Through one of her conversations with Paula, she determined that the above terms would help her in this effort. Subsequent project steps included writing and editing drafts of what she described as a "lengthy paper" on the series.

In preparing for the Final Product and Presentation stage of her project, Reidun looked over a packet of suggestions of effective presentation methods. The packet included a checklist to help her prepare her presentation of her paper and a template of an evaluation form that attendees would use to assess the presentation. Reidun presented her ten-page, single-spaced treatise to an audience of HSRA students and staff members. She introduced her paper with the following: "When I started this project, I had the idea of writing an intermediate *Harry Potter for Dummies* type paper, outlining at least a half-dozen characters, musing on what exactly makes this series so popular, and finally, writing one very long report on all six books (which total 3,341 pages so far, in case you ever had an itch to know). However, upon reading the fifth and sixth installments in the series, my whole grasp of *Harry Potter*, and this project, changed drastically."[18]

She went on to explain that she was so disappointed with the sixth book in the series that it changed her perspective and, while she still believed the series was good literature and anxiously awaited the final installment, her analysis of Rowling's work had shifted. Some attendees of her presentation were diehard Harry Potter fans who agreed with her analysis, other fans disagreed, and other attendees played devil's advocate, questioning the quality of the entire series and pushing Reidun to defend the books.

Finally, in the Reflection stage Reidun looked back at the goals she had set and the validations she had hoped to complete and to assess her progress. Ultimately, in order for her to receive credit, Paula and her advisor had to sign off on each validation. Through the project, "Harry Potter and the Senior Who Needs to Graduate," Reidun received credit for state standards such as "Reading, understanding, responding to, analyzing and appreciating fiction"; "Writing with attention to audience, organization, focus and quality of ideas"; and "Applying standard English conventions while writing."

Reidun didn't read Herman Melville or J. D. Salinger while at HSRA. She loved Harry Potter, so she read J. K. Rowling.

Whether or not the Harry Potter series is of the same literary merit as *The Catcher in the Rye* is an argument best left for another book— perhaps one by Reidun—but regardless of the outcome, it is clear that through her passion for Harry Potter and the assistance of the staff at HSRA, she developed new skills, such as thinking critically, researching, dreaming up a product, developing a timeline, tracking down resources to complete the project, and presenting her work publicly. These skills and experiences will be far more crucial to her success in life than having crammed enough of *Moby Dick* to pass a quiz when she was eighteen.

Many projects are not as similar to conventional schoolwork as Reidun's paper; however, examining this particular project brings the distinguishing benefits of project-based learning into relief.

On a superficial level, Reidun wrote a paper on a book—a similar task to one she might have been given had she attended any other high school in the Twin Cities. In most of those schools, the paper would have been generated and assessed in a typical sequence: an entire cohort of students would be assigned the same book to read, they would receive the same guidelines for writing a paper, the students who completed the assignment would submit their papers to the teacher on the same date, and then wait to receive numeric or letter grades, which would most likely be the last anyone ever saw or thought about the paper.

Reidun, on the other hand, had much more control and responsibility. She could select a subject about which she was passionate. She was then able to craft a project around the specific set of skills she wanted to learn so that she could articulately defend the series and demonstrate ability in learning areas that would help her advance to graduation. And it all happened on a timeline that made sense given her other work and the nature of the project.

It may have taken Reidun a long time to read 3,341 pages and that was fine, as long as she was communicating with her advisor about her progress. If the last book in the series had been released while she was working on the project, she could have elected to extend her timeline to incorporate the final volume.

The paper Reidun generated was not just viewed in private by a teacher but vetted publicly; she had to be prepared to explain and defend her work, and it mattered because it could influence an audience of peers and elders. In the end, her assessment came from herself, her peers, and her educators. Instead of receiving a letter grade, her specific accomplishments were validated.

To live healthy and fulfilling lives, young people must graduate prepared to create, relate, and innovate. These are the types of skills that individually crafted and conducted projects build for students. Through project-based learning, students practice examining problems, thinking critically, and developing resourceful solutions—crucial skills in a world of constant change.

## REAL MOTIVATION

Critically analyzing something and taking action to change it takes a lot more energy and commitment than filling out worksheets or sitting through classes. There will inevitably be setbacks, moments when students run into challenges they have never encountered before. But just because almost all of the students at HSRA have dropped out, been kicked out, or otherwise disengaged from previous schools doesn't mean that they are not capable of or should not be expected to produce work of extremely high quality.

Although it can be counterproductive to blast students with elusive expectations the moment they walk through the door, it is a mistake not to quickly challenge them with real work that matters and that will be seen and used by others. Once students feel respected and that their work matters in the real world, expectations can be ratcheted up. As teacher and education coach Ron Berger explains in his book *An Ethic of Excellence*, holding high expectations for students' work and supporting them in generating work that meets those expectations can actually *cause* their self-esteem to blossom.

Some teachers get it backwards and think that if students are struggling and lack confidence, the only way to keep them engaged is by taking it easy on them. In fact, when an educator pushes a student to "make discoveries that impress their classmates, solve problems as part of the group, put together projects that are admired by others, [and] produce work of real quality, a new self-image as a proud student will emerge."[19]

Charlie Hustle is a senior at HSRA. After falling three years behind his age group at Park Center High School, Charlie left.

Charlie's primary focus when he enrolled at HSRA two years ago was to catch up on academics, so that he could graduate high school before he was in his twenties. But once he began attending, Charlie became involved in Click4Life, a partnership HSRA had formed with State Farm Insurance.

State Farm came to HSRA for assistance with a seatbelt safety campaign. A few dozen students were interested in working with the insurance company to raise awareness and campaign for better public policies regarding seatbelt safety. Each student found specific roles and responsibilities and received different validations for his or her participation.

Together, the crew researched issues related to seatbelt use, organized a youth summit on teen driver safety, advocated at the state house for stronger laws mandating that seat belts be worn by all passengers at all times, created an album about driving safety, organized performances and events, and traveled to Philadelphia and Nashville to network with other people who shared their commitment to these issues.

Last year, the primary seatbelt law that the students were advocating for was passed. And the partnership between HSRA and State Farm is still growing. Charlie and the other students involved do not have to go through HSRA staff members to interact with State Farm personnel; they call them directly to discuss products and plans. The work they do matters—to people within the school, to State Farm, and to the safety of their communities.

Several staff members noticed that Charlie liked to draw and recommended that he also join the Sweat Equity Enterprises Design workshop. Because this workshop was created in partnership with fashion designer Marc Ecko's nonprofit organization, the workshop teaches design principles through projects for actual clients, such as Ecko's own street-wear company. Students have periodic videoconferences and meetings with designers, with the intention that designs from the group will be marketed and sold. This means the standards and stakes for students are high.

Charlie remembers entering the workshop: "I instantly needed to learn," he pauses to correct himself, "no, *master* Photoshop, InDesign, and Illustrator." Charlie recalls that peers joined the workshop interested in learning how to use the high-end computers and design software to customize their MySpace backgrounds, but they were quickly pulled into designing T-shirts and logos.

"I still got friends who go to normal school," Charlie says with pride, "who'll be like, 'How you do that? Where you learn that?'" In addition to the real-world nature of the projects that the Sweat Equity workshop takes on, the fancy software they have at their fingertips, and their connection to a design celebrity, Charlie attributes his rapidly developing skills and self-confidence to the way staff at HSRA interact with him. "They treat us like business partners. They treat us like adults."

As students engage in projects that matter to them and get a taste of generating high-quality products, they increasingly see value in the school as an institution. It can take some time for students to unlearn a decade of authoritarian schooling, but once students feel empowered and confident, taking on high levels of challenge becomes less intimidating and more desirable.

"Some people are skeptical about the limitations of tapping into something relevant for students to get them excited to learn," says Paula Anderson, HSRA's director of academics. But while a student's attention may initially have been sparked by music, fashion, or a social justice issue, "Once they develop personal goals and things they'd like to see change in their community, learning algebra becomes relevant, if for no other reason than just to the point of being smarter and moving forward toward their personal goals."

## TO BE KNOWN

For many students, just hearing the word "teacher" evokes repulsion. Teachers have been known as authority figures charged with controlling young peoples' behavior, while assessing their intelligence and, too frequently, punishing them. One student at HSRA referred to past teachers as "resentful." Another said her teachers were "going through the motions to collect a check," and others mentioned that their teachers had been afraid of them.

Similarly, many reported that their past guidance counselors had provided little guidance. Often their caseloads were so large that they did not know students' names. Their role was to address computer glitches in class schedules and assist the fraction of students who both made it to senior year and repeatedly expressed an interest in applying to college.

And despite the mnemonic for remembering how to spell the end of the word "principal," for HSRA students, past principals have rarely been friends, or even friendly. They were just teachers who made it a step up the rude chain. Time and again, principals served as the judge and jury that exiled students from their previous schools with little due process.

HSRA does not have teachers, guidance counselors, or a principal. From orientation through graduation, these are titles that students do not hear. This is an intentional cue that the kinds of antagonistic dynamics described above will not exist at the school.

What kinds of relationships between adults and students replace the adversarial ones that too many students have come to expect in educational institutions? At HSRA, the main point of contact students have with staff is their *advisor*.

Upon enrolling at the school, each student is assigned to an advisory, which they are a part of for the duration of their tenure at the school. Students do not switch to new advisories at the end of each year. They develop an ongoing relationship with their advisor, who builds an understanding of their strengths, passions, needs, and challenges.

"She comes to my boxing matches," says one student about his advisor. "She started going to my church," says another. A third student adds that she used to be shy, but her advisor noticed this and "started making me get on stage at community meeting to announce little things like trips." At first this student felt nervous. "Now they can't shut me up!" she says with pride.

"An advisory system is the best structure to improve a school's atmosphere and culture and make an already small school feel even smaller and more personalized," explains Dennis Littky, cofounder of the Met Schools and Big Picture Learning.[20] Littky and his colleagues began using advisories in the 1970s. "In my experience, having advisories affects everything, from reducing vandalism to increasing parent participation to decreasing dropouts."[21]

Littky is a personal friend of TC, and the Met Schools were influential to TC and his team as they designed HSRA. What Littky, TC, and other educators have seen is that "Just when most adolescents are pulling away from their own families, the high school advisory and the advisor can take on some of the roles that are necessary, literally, for the kids' survival."[22]

"Being an advisor is not just a euphemism for being a teacher," explains Uncle Phil. "It's coaching [students] on a lot of things. And being there for them." When one student was hit by a car, her advisor was the first one to the hospital. When another student got locked up, his first phone call was to his advisor, and when he was released, he stopped by HSRA before he went home.

Many teachers in traditional schools see five different cohorts of students every day. Each of these classes may contain as many as thirty students and the entire schedule can change as often as midyear. This means teachers commonly work with anywhere from one hundred to three hundred students in a single year!

In such a context, how can one be expected to notice, remember, and build curriculum around Chantel's passion for singing? Whose responsibility is it to take the time to learn that Jason's family has been evicted and help him find a solution to this threat to his well-being?

Due to funding cutbacks, advisory sizes at HSRA have recently grown to as many as thirty students. To be most effective, advisories should be half that size. But even thirty is a more manageable number of students for a staff member to develop meaningful relationships with than three hundred.

Over a one- to four-year period, advisors can get to know students' passions, challenges, and idiosyncrasies. Good advisors can quickly identify an article or opportunity that would interest a particular student. They can see the difference between a student being in a funky mood because she is having a bad day and when something bigger is going wrong in her life. And they are likely to know how to defuse a situation with a student that in another context would lead to disciplinary action. They know which family members and friends to call for assistance. And they know how to get that student plugged back into an activity, as soon as she's ready.

The advantage to structuring schools in advisories goes beyond the trust that students develop with adults. Advisories also provide each student with a small group of peers within the school.

Students at HSRA spend at least eight hours each week with their advisory. They share not only academic pursuits but also triumphs and challenges from life outside of school. They give each other wake-up calls, talk each other out of fights, and throw parties for each other's graduations. Students grow close with one another, providing each other support as they work to achieve goals, calling each other out when they stray from the paths to success they have laid out for themselves, and feeling pride for one another's achievements.

In this context, lesbian, gay, bisexual, and transgender students are less prone to the harassment that is pervasive in larger, more anonymous school environments.[23] While some homophobia permeates the campus, students develop friendships in their advisories, regardless of sexual orientation. "It's not like there's no comments," advisor Kowanna Powell Anderson says, referring to a young man in her advisory who sometimes attends school in drag. "But it's never like nobody is ostracized. They all hang out. They all go to parties together. They all spend the night at the same place."

Because students attend HSRA for different durations, some students grow closer with their advisory mates than others. A student who is at the school for four years naturally has more time to bond with his or her peers than a student who arrives at HSRA at age nineteen only in need of a few credits. But students in both circumstances can have strong ties to their advisories.

Some students who come to HSRA late in their high school career have felt so alienated at past schools that advisory is the most important part of HSRA for them. Some are trying to break ties with former friends who are caught up in gangs, drugs, and prostitution, and they are actively looking to build relationships with peers on a positive path. At a maximum enrollment of 250 students, the whole school is small enough that some students look at it as "one big advisory where strong friendships develop across the school."

Ultimately, for many students and staff members, HSRA is not just a school, a recording studio, or a community. It is *a family*.

## FAMILY'S VALUE

For a school community, being family means caring for each other through tough times. Often what students need is intense, personal, emotional support. Visitors to the school have remarked that students seem calmer in the morning and noticeably more irritable and unruly toward the end of the day. HSRA's director of development, Tony Simmons, suggests that this is because as students get closer to having to leave the safe and supportive environment of the school, they grow anxious.

Tony's statement is based on the knowledge that most HSRA students have challenging circumstances waiting for them beyond the walls of the school. Each year, approximately 30 percent have been homeless at some time within the school year. In the 2006–2007 school year, 63 percent of the students at HSRA self-reported that they were on probation or parole. Twenty percent reported having at least one child and/or being pregnant. Eight percent reported being the victim of abuse.

It is not unusual to find a student and a staff member tucked away in one of the small offices discussing a life challenge that a student is experiencing.

The culture among the school's staff—from advisors to maintenance people to administrators—is that part of working at the school, regardless of job title, is to know students well, care about them, and show it. Over the past several years, there have always been at least seven staff members (out of a total staff of approximately forty) who were HSRA graduates, with a personal understanding of the challenges that students at the school face. Several other staff members grew up having similar experiences and can relate on a personal level to the circumstances of students' lives.

HSRA also has a full-time social worker on staff to support students who are in difficult situations. Although Tabitha Wheeler is trained and licensed as a social worker, she refers to herself as a "youth advocate" to avoid the automatic distrust that many students and families have developed for anyone with the "social worker" title.

It is Tabitha's role to not only counsel students but also to hook them up with support services for additional assistance that the school cannot provide. Students in need of safe, stable housing are connected with Street Works, a local agency that helps find living arrangements for students and provides them with gift cards for food and clothing. Students struggling with drug addictions are connected to organizations such as African American Family Services for counseling and support. Additional partnerships connect students with job opportunities, internships, sex education, and life skills.

When a student is confronted with a challenging issue, such as getting kicked out of his house, Tabitha does not just refer him to an outside agency and then move on to the next. Her experience has taught her that many young people will not feel comfortable following up with the level of persistence that it takes to get the services they need. So she begins by listening to the student's situation and presenting options.

Sometimes a student's needs require both immediate and long-term solutions. If a student comes to her with nowhere to stay that night, she is prepared with a bag of toiletries and clothing, a list of phone numbers for shelters, as well as some money for food and payphone calls.

If the student wants to seek assistance from an external agency, Tabitha and the student will rehearse calling the agency. In some cases, when students feel particularly uncomfortable or are not being treated with respect by an agency, Tabitha will get on the phone with them. And, in certain instances, she will go with a student to check out a shelter and make sure the student feels safe there or she will join their first meeting with a case manager. Verbally and through her actions, Tabitha tells students, "I'll work as hard as you do to sort out whatever's going on."

By brokering students' relationships with external agencies and providing interpersonal emotional support, the HSRA staff offers targeted, tangible assistance. The school invests a huge amount of energy in this work, and it keeps many students enrolled through tumultuous times. In the event that a student gets overwhelmed and stops attending for a while, she or he is warmly welcomed when she or he returns.

Over a fall weekend in 2008, two HSRA students were held at gunpoint. Word got to TC that they were telling people around school that they were going to retaliate, so he invited them into his office and asked them what was going on. One of them recounted the confrontation from the weekend and concluded, "When you pull heat out on me, you bodied yourself."

TC asked point-blank, "So you gonna kill him?"

"I'm not sayin' nothin,'" the young man replied, avoiding eye contact.

"You're not saying nothing, but we understand what you're saying," TC replied.

Instead of getting frightened and immediately expelling the boys or calling the police, as many schools would do, TC tried to relate to the young men and reason with them. "I've never had a gun pulled on me," he declared at one point, but then he paused and thought about it for a moment. "Well, actually I have, but that situation was different . . ."

TC brought in "Big Layne" Bellamy, a childhood friend of his, who now serves as the school's facilities manager, and Jonathan Moore, the dean of students with sixteen years of experience as a corrections officer. They each took turns expressing how much they cared about the young men and how concerned they were about the boys causing harm to others and themselves.

After over an hour of trying every rhetorical approach they could come up with, TC summed up his and his colleagues' sentiments, "We're your people. . . . Even if you fuck up, end up dead or in prison, I'm still gonna love you. But I'm gonna be like, I tried to tell the brother . . ."

Love is demonstrated by different staff members at HSRA in different ways. When a student wants a sympathetic ear, a box of tissues, or a hug, he or she goes to Tabitha's office. Offering comfort or congratulations in the form of a hug may seem commonplace, but in recent years schools across the country, including in Minnesota, have banned hugging.[24]

Many students at HSRA have histories of physical and sexual abuse, and staff members at HSRA are trained to be thoughtful about issues that may come up around physical contact, but they hug students regularly. Students do the same for staff and each other.

But some students don't want hugs. A student looking for "tough love" can go to Big Layne for a stern lecture. Even when students are upset to the point of screaming or fighting, they will often end up near a staff member who they know can help, whether "help" means getting them out of the building for a few minutes or breaking up the fight before it starts. Each day at HSRA there are examples of these sorts of organic parental and sibling-like caretaking.

Routine elements of HSRA's structure and schedule encourage healthy familial behaviors. Every day after lunch a short session called Touchback provides a time for members of the community to make announcements, share performances, and air congratulations and concerns. Weekly community meetings serve as extended opportunities for students and staff to engage in dialogues about past and upcoming issues and events. Problems are not allowed to boil beneath the surface. No matter how uncomfortable a topic, it is addressed.

Community meetings have delved into topics ranging from keeping common spaces clean to gender relations within the school to how to properly honor the life and mourn the death of a beloved staff member. All sides of issues are heard and considered.

For instance, when security guards from the nearby McDonald's approached HSRA administrators to complain about student behavior in the fast-food restaurant during lunch, they were invited to attend a community meeting. They were welcomed to present their concerns and students had the opportunity to describe their frustrations with the treatment they received from the security guards. These community dialogues can be difficult for all involved, but they can also serve to keep students and staff honest and open with each other.

Feeling like a part of a family can be a powerful antidote to the lure of gangs, which have become a path to self-destruction for far too many young geniuses. A research review on gang violence and prevention found that young people join gangs looking for love, structure, discipline, belonging, commitment, recognition, power, companionship, training, excitement, activities, a sense of self-worth, a place of acceptance, physical safety, and family traditions.[25]

Many schools offer structure, discipline, training, activities, and at least a moderate level of physical safety. Some schools also provide recognition, excitement, a sense of self-worth, and traditions. Very few schools offer belonging, commitment, power, companionship, a place of acceptance, and love.

The High School for Recording Arts creates a sense of belonging and a culture of love so powerful that some young people come to trade in their gang bandanas for "All Access" studio passes. The chance to explore musical production and other passions are a big part of the draw, but in the end, what matters most to many students is not whether they have access to beat machines and microphones, it is whether the school is theirs—whether they love and belong to it and whether it loves and belongs to them.

## NOTES

1. School staff members and students are referred to by their first names and/or nicknames throughout this chapter, because that is how people refer to each other at the school.

2. William Duff, *An Essay on Original Genius* (New York: Garland, 1970), 6.

3. Adam Mansbach, "On Lit Hop," in *Total Chaos: The Art and Aesthetics of Hip-Hop*, ed. Jeff Chang (New York: Basic Civitas, 2006), 93.

4. Jeff Chang, *Can't Stop Won't Stop: A History of the Hip-Hop Generation* (New York: Picador, 2005), 97.

5. Mansbach, "On Lit Hop," 93.

6. Nelson George, *Hip Hop America* (New York: Penguin, 1998), 14–15.

7. The Fo-Show's name is a reference to Studio 4, the company that provides education management and studio services to the school. It is also a reference to the school's four guiding principles: family, community, respect, and education.

8. Etta R. Hollins, *Culture in School Learning: Revealing the Deep Meaning* (Mahwah, N.J.: Lawrence Erlbaum, 1996), 2.

9. Etta R. Hollins and Eileen I. Oliver, eds., *Pathways to Success in School: Culturally Responsive Teaching* (Mahwah, N.J.: Lawrence Erlbaum, 1999), xiii.

10. An HSRA alumnus pursuing a career as a rapper points out with pride that he is the only artist approaching record labels with such an image on his diploma.

11. The term "Pick-Me-Up" is borrowed from the Big Picture Learning school design. At Big Picture schools, Pick Me Ups do not serve as artist showcases but rather as all-school events where some type of engaging/energizing presentation occurs. For more information, see www.bigpicture.org.

12. Madison Park, "Falling Asleep in Class? Blame Biology," *CNN*, December 15, 2008, http://www.cnn.com/2008/HEALTH/12/12/sleep.teenagers .school/index.html (accessed December 16, 2010).

13. Alexander Salagaev, "Juvenile Delinquency," in *World Youth Report 2003: The Global Situation of Young People* (New York: United Nations, 2004), 201.

14. High School for Recording Arts, Course Catalog Semester 2, 2009, Version 2.1, January 2009, 8.

15. This phrase refers to the frequently referenced quote from Mahatma Gandhi: "Be the change you wish to see in the world."

16. High School for Recording Arts, "Competency-Based Graduation Plan," 6.

17. For more information on the Buck Institute for Education, see http://www.bie.org/.

18. Reidun Saxerud, "Harry Potter and the Senior Who Needs to Graduate," 1.

19. Ron Berger, *An Ethic of Excellence: Building a Culture of Craftmanship with Students* (Portsmouth, N.H.: Heinemann, 2003), 65.

20. Dennis Littky and Samantha Grabelle, *The Big Picture: Education Is Everyone's Business* (Alexandria, Va.: ASCD, 2002), 62.

21. Littky and Grabelle, *The Big Picture*, 64.

22. Littky and Grabelle, *The Big Picture*, 63.

23. Multiple studies show that approximately 90 percent of lesbian, gay, bisexual, and transgender students in this country experience harassment at school. See, for example, Elizabeth M. Diaz and Joseph G. Kosciw, "Shared Differences: The Experiences of Lesbian, Gay, Bisexual and Transgender Students of Color in Our Nation's Schools," *GLSEN* (2009): 2.

24. Mike Celizic, "Schools Jumping on the Hug Ban-Wagon," *TodayShow .com*, October 2 2007, http://www.msnbc.msn.com/id/21097673/ (accessed December 16, 2010).

25. Mary H. Lees, Mary Deen, and Louise Parker, "Research Review: Gang Violence and Prevention," Focus Adolescent Services, http://www.focusas.com/Gangs.html (accessed December 16, 2010).

# ② 

# A DAY'S WORK

This is my preparation to my destination
And I'm a stay committed even through the complications
I'm a stay strong an' keep my head up
I'm a give it my all until I've had enough
'Cause if I dream big I know that I can make it
This is the real me welcome to my inspiration.

—Lil C

The High School for Recording Arts (HSRA) is so unconventional that it can be hard for people who have only spent time in more traditional schools to picture how things actually flow on a daily basis.

As people who have never seen these elements in a school hear about the recording studios, the student-run record label, the hours, the trips, the advisory model, and all of the different ways that students can earn credits, a common reaction is: This all sounds amazing, but what does it actually look like day in and day out? How do students know what they are supposed to be doing, where they are supposed to be, and when? How do staff members budget their time and priorities?

The best way to illustrate the rhythm and flow of the school is to provide a snapshot of one day in the life of an HSRA student. This chapter follows Cassandra "Lil C" Sherry-Rojas, who is in her junior year.[1] When

Lil C enrolled at HSRA, she had never rapped in public before. Three years later, she has won awards for her stage performances, rocked venues from local talent shows to Los Angeles, and appeared in a music video to raise money for Haitian earthquake recovery efforts that has been viewed 400,000 times.

Lil C balances her passion as an emcee with a serious approach to her academic pursuits. Some HSRA students are highly motivated when it comes to their projects and have no interest in music. Others are passionate about music but drag their feet on academic responsibilities. Although Lil C's equilibrium of the academic and musical components of HSRA's program may not be typical, it provides a rich perspective of the HSRA experience.

## LIL C'S JOURNEY TO HSRA

In a quiet residential development called Lafayette East, seventeen-year-old Cassandra "Lil C" Sherry-Rojas is getting ready for school. She settles on a white hoody with a large silver Adidas logo, black shelltoes with white stripes, a Yankees hat with gray stripes, and red basketball shorts that hang out over the top of sagging gray jeans.

Lil C steps out the front door and walks past a row of recently constructed duplexes that look just like hers. After spending the first nine years of her life in what she described as "bad neighborhoods" in St. Paul, Lil C's mother arranged a move to a first-ring suburb so that they could enjoy a more peaceful life in a safer area.

Though South St. Paul is only ten miles from where Lil C spent her younger years, the move required her to make a cultural leap. While she'd had fun and gotten good grades in elementary school, by the time she was a freshman at South St. Paul High School, she dreaded attending.

"Man, I hated that school—they were racist! The principal wanted to kick me out for no reason," Lil C recalls. Within the first few months of her freshmen year, she was barely showing up, which further increased the antagonism she felt from school staff.

When Lil C heard about HSRA, she jumped at the chance to enroll. She now travels three hours round trip each day to attend the school.

The public Metro bus she rides does not take the highway. As it dips in and out of traffic to pick up passengers, Lil C listens to music on her MP3 player and looks out the window as tree nurseries, shopping centers, steakhouses, and soccer fields give way to the low-slung industrial, retail, and residential buildings of St. Paul. Switching buses in downtown St. Paul, Lil C rides the #16 up University Avenue, eventually hopping off at Vandalia Street and walking ten minutes to the school.

After being buzzed through the front doors of HSRA and saying "What's up?" to "Monsta Codie" Wilson, an alumnus-turned-youth-worker who now serves as school security, Lil C stops to greet "Uncle Phil" Winden, the studio director: "What up, Phil?!"

"Hey, Lil C," Phil responds from a chair positioned directly in front of the recording studio, his laptop flipped open on his lap.

"I need some studio time, bro!" Lil C tells him.

"Okay," Phil says, "come see me this afternoon. We'll see what's open."

Lil C agrees, spins, and hops across the hall ten feet to the door of her advisory.


## KDA ADVISORY

While most advisories at HSRA are in the giant open room down the hall, two advisories share this thousand-square-foot space. Because the advisories share the room, they have informally merged. The two advisors, Darryl "Duke" Gibson and Kowanna Powell Anderson (whose first initials together form the name of the advisory) share the responsibility of advising the forty students who are in their collective group.

Lil C bursts in and makes a loop around the room, greeting students seated at computers that line two of the walls and others lounging on couches. Some are eating a breakfast of eggs, hash browns, and sausages provided for free by the school. Duke looks up from his computer to welcome Lil C as she approaches. Kowanna is collecting miscellaneous sheets of paper from a long rectangular table and smaller circular table that form an exclamation point on the opposite side of the room.

"Good morning, Lil C," Kowanna says as she straightens chairs around the table.

"G'morning!" Lil C shouts back.

HSRA's lead advisor, Mike Conway walks into the advisory with a new advisee who is interested in a workshop called Money Makes Money that Mike, Kowanna, and Dario Otero, the school's special education transitional advisor, offer. As Lil C chats with friends, Kowanna introduces herself to the new student and asks him about his interests.

"Cars," he says. After a bit more conversation, she gives him a packet titled "Is This Business Right for Me? A Personal Assessment Workbook," which is part of a curriculum from the Neighborhood Development Center. She asks him to use the packet to test his interest in pursuing a profession related to automobiles before coming to the next meeting of the workshop.

As Mike and the advisee leave, an alumna, Totiana Adams, comes in and wishes Kowanna a belated happy birthday. They chat for a bit and then Kowanna asks, "Okay, are we gonna do this?" Totiana raises a video camera into Kowanna's line of sight, and Kowanna says, "Oh, you're filming?!"

Totiana explains that she intends to use segments of their conversation for a play she has been working on. She has been conducting interviews to capture real women's stories, which she plans to incorporate into a performance that "speaks for the unspoken."

Lil C and other students have been hanging around the room talking, but some start to gather around to watch Kowanna's interview. She does nothing to dissuade them. One of the students warns, "Careful what you say, ten million people could see this!"

"What y'all scared of ten million people for?" asks Totiana. "I hope the whole world gets to see this play!" She returns to Kowanna, "Okay, tell me about your life growing up."

Without skipping a beat, Kowanna speaks directly to the camera, "I was raised in Chicago until I was twelve, when my family moved to Minnesota. I was the oldest of four girls and we were raised by my grandparents and my mom. I was closest to my grandfather. My mom was more like a sister, 'til I got pregnant and then our relationship bloomed and grew to more of a mother/daughter relationship."

Totiana asks about Kowanna's family's financial status while she was growing up. "I didn't think about money in Chicago, but when we moved to Minnesota I needed money, and got a job. . . . For me, money was never about material things. It was about security. I was insecure growing up—"

"What were you insecure about?" Totiana interjects.

In front of students—past and current—Kowanna exposes some of her personal insecurities. "My hair. I woulda changed my body shape— skinny girls were not 'in.'"

In talking about turning points in her life, Kowanna describes an HSRA-sponsored trip she took to Guatemala when she herself was a student at the school. Seeing people with no material possessions smiling and sharing with strangers was profound. She returned to Minnesota with a new outlook and revised priorities.

The conversation continues, touching on personal topics ranging from Kowanna's career trajectory to her marriage of ten years. Kowanna answers everything unswervingly—even the most personal questions about family and sex.

Without a bell or a formal announcement, the group has transitioned from informally greeting each other to the half hour advisory block that occurs each morning. The tone of the room has shifted, from frenetic interactions to focused attention. Duke works quietly at his desk, allowing attention in the room to rest on Kowanna. At one point during the interview, the room phone rings. A student answers in a hushed tone: "Kowanna's advisory. . . . Okay, I'll let her know."

This is an interview for an alumna's play, but Kowanna has chosen to conduct it in front of her advisees. It has become a learning moment, an opportunity to be vulnerable in front of her students. Kowanna's honesty and openness with her students adds to the atmosphere of safety in sharing that is embedded in the school's culture.

Students who have been burned repeatedly by social service agencies can be extremely reluctant to open up about even the most basic aspects of their lives, but if an adult is willing to disclose her family history and fears, students may be more willing to share and move toward healing. The fact that Kowanna has experienced some of the same challenges as many of her students and is willing to speak openly about them serves to normalize narratives that other schools and social service agencies deem dysfunctional—or won't even acknowledge.

Kowanna's candidness about her past honors hip-hop culture's emphasis on the importance of origin and identity. One of the first questions many hip-hop fans ask when hearing music by a new artist is, "Who is this?" Next question: "Where's s/he from?" A rapper's identity is a key piece of how his or her music is interpreted and judged.

Students do the same thing with their educators. It is not that an advisor has to have a particular narrative to garner respect. Sometimes commonalities between a student and advisor's background can facilitate trust and connection, but more importantly, teachers must be willing to honestly represent who they are and where they're from.

Totiana wraps up the interview with a final request: "Okay, tell 'em who you are!"

In so many ways Kowanna already has, but she obliges: "I'm Kowanna Powell, I'm thirty years old. I'm an academic advisor at HSRA and Studio Fo'. And you know what the Fo' fo': family, community, respect, and education. That's how it go down."[2]

## BLOCK ONE: PROJECT WORK

Students are spread out around the advisory room. Some are seated at computers working on Project Excellence, HSRA's in-house software program designed to help students track their progress toward demonstrating competence in each of the twelve learning areas required for graduation.[3]

Two students seated next to each other have PowerPoint presentations open—one is showing the other how to add a special effect so that when slides advance they appear to fly out toward the audience before landing in place. Another student has the software program iWeb open and is adding content to her digital portfolio, while another is on MySpace listening to music on his headphones.

At the last computer, a student is flipping between celebrity gossip websites. Perhaps she intended to start working on Project Excellence or her digital portfolio and just got sucked into a juicy string of blog posts about Mo'Nique's beef with Oprah and Steven Seagal's alleged assault of Ray Charles's granddaughter. She would not be the first person, after all, to have fallen victim to the powerful distractions of the World Wide Web. Twenty minutes are lost—a casualty of the freedom that accompanies independent learning.

It would be easy for an observer to jump to conclusions about who's working and who's wasting time, but things are not always as they seem at project-based learning schools. In this particular instance, the young woman surfing cyber tabloids is actually conducting research for a project on rumors. The young man on MySpace may also be working, though it's possible he is procrastinating. Surface appearances can be deceptive when people are engaged in individualized projects, particularly when the canon of what is being mastered is opened up to include contemporary communication tools, current media, and other new forms of literacy.

The students who are not using computers are seated on couches and chairs. Two are reading stacks of photocopied papers; another is looking through a crate of books; the other has headphones on and his eyes closed.

It is hard to imagine what project this young man is working on—though there certainly are some projects that could necessitate such an activity. More likely he just needed a minute to chill out. Giving him the space to do that is what HSRA staff refer to as "deliberate patience."

Many of the young people enrolled at the school have a lot going on in their lives. From late-night jobs to abusive situations at home to homelessness, there are numerous reasons students may arrive at school exhausted or on edge. For some, it is the only place they can relax. So while it does not help anyone if laziness goes unaddressed, staff members temper demands that students constantly be on task with deliberate patience.

A young person cannot treat the school as a place to sleep and socialize through the week. But if a particular student needs a few minutes to recuperate, meditate, or do whatever else he needs to do to get his mind right, his advisor can give him that space. And unlike most schools where social promotion and cheating make it possible for students to sleep through classes and still pass, the longer it takes an HSRA student to get started on her work, the longer it takes her to graduate.

Deliberate patience is a deeply engrained part of HSRA's culture. When the school's founder, David "TC" Ellis, was a student at an alternative public school, he routinely crawled into a loft and slept. It was only when one day a teacher woke him and asked him if he wanted to learn how to protect his money that his passion for learning ignited.

HSRA has tried to institutionalize this sort of intervention without becoming overbearing to the students who just need ten minutes to clear
their heads.

Lil C is not one of those students. Like several of her advisory mates,
who are spread out around the school working on projects, in workshops, or in meetings, Lil C is making moves. Her first stop is TC's office, where Tony Simmons, HSRA's director of development, is seated
at a round table.

"Wassup, Tony?" Lil C says as she pops through the door.

"Lil C," Tony declares with enthusiasm, looking up from his laptop.

"Tony! Can I get those photos, bro?" Lil C asks, referring to a few
dozen photographs of her that a professional photographer recently
took for the cover of *City Pages*, the Twin Cities' preeminent weekly
paper on local news and culture. Tony has digital versions of the photos
and Lil C wants copies.

"Where's my timeline?" he says with a smile.

"Aww, man," Lil C says. "I been trying to get it done, but I just been
focused on my other project."

"That's cool," Tony responds. "I'm not asking for a finished project,
but you said you'd get me the timeline for getting it done. I've been
telling people about it. I want to be able to share it with some people. It
could help open up some opportunities for you."

"I don't even have the project proposal with me," C says.

Tony reaches in his backpack and pulls out a photocopied sheet of
paper. "That's why I had you make me a copy," he tells her. "Here, go
make a copy of this—no, make two copies—and put together a timeline
for me. If you let this go too long, it's not gonna happen."

Lil C accepts the document from Tony, but instead of leaving to make
copies, she stands at the table with him and reviews it. The project being
discussed is tentatively titled "A Picture Is Worth a Thousand Words,
but to a High School Student, What Is an Article Really Worth?" Her
plan is to conduct research and write a response to the recent cover
story in *City Pages*.

Lil C and Tony discuss the outline she crafted for the piece. The first
few paragraphs will be about whether the three students featured in
the article felt it was accurate. To write this, she will have to interview
the other two students who were profiled alongside her in the article.

The following few paragraphs will summarize audience reactions, which she will collect through additional interviews or surveys. The final paragraphs will focus on how the article affected Lil C personally.

The press frequently portrays young people, particularly urban youth of color, in a negative light. HSRA's individualized curriculum allows students to critically engage with the way the media represents them. In this case, Lil C was profiled in a cover story that cast her in a positive light while disclosing details about painful personal chapters from her past.

Regardless of how Lil C felt about the article, shouldn't she have the opportunity to respond? A great English teacher at a traditional high school might encourage something like this from a student, perhaps offering extra credit. At HSRA Lil C's critical response can be a central piece of her academic work.

Otis,[4] a student wearing a button-down shirt and sweater vest, knocks on the open door and then steps in to ask if it's all right for him to leave early because "G-Unit's manager is in town and I've gotta go meet with him." Tony tells him to check in with his advisor about this plan.

After the interruption in their conversation, Lil C changes the topic to another project of hers, one that she feels has momentum at the moment. "I'm working on a book and I need y'all to do a survey," she announces.

"If I get my timeline . . . ," Tony says, smiling again.

TC comes in, peeps the conversation, and adds his own agenda item: "We're tryna get you to take advantage of PSEO," he says to Lil C, "get you some free college credits while you in high school."[5]

"But I wanna go to McNally," Lil C says, referring to McNally Smith, a college in the Twin Cities known for its music program.

"So this is a chance to get some of your other credits out of the way and get a little bit of that college experience," TC persists.

"Can I do psychology?" she asks.

"I don't know why not," TC says. "But you need to get the ball rolling on that so that you can get in some classes for the fall and then some more next spring. You could have a nice piece of college under your belt by the time you graduate up outta here."

Lil C agrees to look into college courses and heads off to make copies of her outline and survey.

The survey is seven pages and contains about seventy-five questions, grouped in categories, such as "Profile," "Relationships," "Favorites," and "Randoms." On the back of the survey is a release form, which—in a few hundred words of legalese—authorizes Lil C to publish the information she collects. She is asking each person who takes the survey to sign a form. Discussing this issue with the school's lawyer and adding this component to the survey was part of her project.

This is one of the strengths of project-based learning: It puts students of any age in a position to develop real expertise. Lil C actually worked with a practicing lawyer to craft a permission form that meets publishing industry standards. As she pursues her interest in music, she will undoubtedly have to deal with copyright issues. This form is something she could use in future writing endeavors. But whether she ultimately settles in the entertainment industry or some other sector, she will enter her future work with a greater level of familiarity and comfort with practical legal issues than she would have if she had remained at South St. Paul High.

Lil C brings the freshly copied surveys to Tony and TC. She explains that she is writing a book on zodiac signs and wants as much original source information as she can collect. She is curious about the correlation between peoples' signs and other aspects of their identities.

"How many of these surveys are you tryna get filled out?" TC asks her.

"As many as I can right now," C responds. "I have twenty completed so far. I'm tryna get five new ones every day. I wanna get at least fifty."

"Okay, I'll fill mine out," Tony says. "But I want to see that timeline before I hand this over to you. I want to show that project to Ice Cube," Tony alludes to a visit that the rapper/film/television star made to HSRA the previous year. "I think it could lead to big things for you."

"Okay," Lil C responds. She dips back out into the hall, stopping each person passing by to ask them if they would be willing to take a survey. Some ask questions about the purpose of the survey and what it entails, most agree, and the freshly printed stack of blank surveys dwindles.


## SOCIAL SKILLS WORKSHOP

No bell rings. No one screams that it is time for Block Two workshops. Dario just passes by Lil C and says, as one might to a friend, "Ay, it's time for Social Skills. You coming?" It's unclear whether he has walked by her because he happened to be passing through the hall on his way to the Another Level Entertainment board room to facilitate the workshop or because he knew C was over there and wanted to cruise by and remind her that it was time.

The school is small enough that if Dario and Tabitha Wheeler, the school's youth advocate who cofacilitates the workshop with him, decided to each walk a loop down a few halls, they could casually tap the shoulder of every student in their workshop in the span of three to four minutes.

The Social Skills workshop consists of a half-dozen students sitting around a table with Tabitha and Dario discussing life challenges and strategies for perseverance. The workshop always begins with each member—including staff—taking a card from a deck of "Tavis Smiley's Empowerment Cards for Survival Living" and discussing the significance of the words on the card to her or himself in the moment.

On this particular day, the conversation centered on one student's frustration about a project that two of her classmates had presented. The project was about violence in the Twin Cities. The presenters had included a slide that had information about the murder of this student's friend. She was frustrated by the inaccuracy of their information.

"Oh my god, I just wanted to *scream*. I really, really wanted to say something to them. It's like, where do you get your information?!" She proceeded to critique the data that they had presented about crime rates and whether they had interpreted it correctly.

The group asked clarifying questions about what she felt and why. Then they suggested some actions she could take—talk to the girls, talk with her advisor, do her own project on her friend's death.

"I don't know, I'm just glad we had group today, " the student said. "I just really needed to get this off my chest because I was, like, dying inside and I swear I wanted to take it out in some negative ways."

In a school where these kinds of dialogues aren't built into the day, this young woman might have lashed out at the two girls who presented the project or she might have bounced from school. Instead, she received empathy, suggestions, and, on the way out the door, a couple of hugs.

## CONCENTRATED MATH

Lil C rolls back into the advisory room. She checks her cell phone and sits down at the long table. Leaning forward on her elbows, she talks with Fat Ellen, a young woman dressed entirely in shades of gray and black with a bus pass tucked into her tank top. There are seven students seated around the table.

One of the girls notices a colorful tattoo peeking out of the bottom of the sleeve of C's hoody. Lil C proudly shows the ink off to everyone at the table. In an elaborate design, her name is spelled out with the letter "i" replaced by a microphone. The mic cord weaves in and out through the letters, as do the lines, notes, and clefs of music notation.

Kowanna is a small woman with a big personality . . . and voice. She announces to the students spread out around the edges of the room working on computers: "Okay, y'all have to save whatever you're working on and log off now!" After giving them a few minutes to wrap up, she uses a software program on her laptop to lock down all the computer monitors, except for two where students who already have all of their math credits are working on Project Excellence.

Kowanna tells the group to continue working on the box and whisker plot graphs that they began the day before, and she asks a student to hand out the related materials. He delivers to the table a stack of four-page printouts that define and explain the graphs.

Next to it he places a stack of sheets titled "Mathematical Analysis of HSRA Absences." The sheet asks students to find the mean, mode, range, and median of absences in their advisory and then to generate a box and whisker plot, which is a graph that depicts the distribution of a set of data by marking the smallest and largest data points and dividing the space between them in a way that visually indicates the dispersion of the remaining data points.

The intention of the assignment, which was created by Mike—who, in addition to his role as lead advisor, also serves as one of the school's math facilitators—is to make a three-way connection between mathematical concepts that are useful for students to know, content that will appear on the state-mandated standardized tests, and something real that affects students' lives and the school community.

Graphing the absences of each student in their advisory (with names removed), students are able to see where they stand on the plot. By answering questions like "Was attendance even across the advisory or were a few students who were absent frequently bringing the mean down?" students and staff are able to develop better strategies to increase attendance.

Kowanna's and Duke's advisories are using the materials Mike developed and—with Mike's blessing and in the presence of one of the school's other certified math facilitators, Barbara Murphy—they have remixed the assignment, replacing the attendance data with reading progress data from the KDA advisories. Since Concentrated Math is conducted within advisories, the group is examining their own data, making it possible for students to analyze their collective and individual reading progress.

Fat Ellen starts singing "A Change Is Gonna Come" by Sam Cooke: "I was . . . bo-o orn by the river . . ."

"In a little tent," another girl chimes in as she takes copies of the printouts.

"You just sat them on the table, I asked you to pass them out," Kowanna says to the student from whom she had requested help distributing materials. He returns to the piles, picks them up, and distributes copies to students around the room who were not seated at the table. Dreamchild is not paying attention when the papers are offered to him.

"Take a paper, Dream," Kowanna urges.

"But I just got here!" Dreamchild responds.

Another student chimes in, "That don't make no sense."

Dreamchild laughs, "I know, but I was needing an excuse!"

Everyone at the table laughs.

Kowanna cuts in, "What you was needing was a math sheet." More laughs. Dreamchild takes papers from the piles and the students' focus returns to the work in front of them.

Three of the students at the table are wearing white earbud headphones, including Lil C, who has hers in one ear. One kid's T-shirt says, "If my music is too loud, you're too old!" The boy next to Lil C, Federal, is looking at his MP3 player as much as he looks at the papers in front of him.

"Did you get 3.5?" C asks Federal, sleeve pushed up on the forearm that carries her tattoo.

"Nah, 3.9," he replies, tilting his MP3 player toward her. He has been using a built-in calculator on the device. It would be easy for Duke, Kowanna, and Mike to assume Federal was using the MP3 player to DJ for himself during Concentrated Math. They have been right near Federal working with other students but haven't said anything to him about his frequent fiddling with the gadget. Maybe he took a moment to select a track or two, but he is also building a habit of using a device he always has on him to solve problems.

Many schools—both traditional and alternative—have policies instructing teachers to confiscate such items from students without pausing to consider how they are being used or how they could be used to further the student's education. There is no doubt that the prevalence of cell phones, MP3 players, and other small electronics can be a huge distraction to students. But given that these contraptions are ubiquitous in their lives outside of school, perhaps it makes sense to help young people develop positive habits, uses, and norms around these devices in school.

Federal and Lil C continue to go back and forth about the process they are each following and the numbers that are resulting. "That's what I got the first time!" Lil C exclaims.

She goes to consult Kowanna about how to determine the median among an even set of numbers. In the course of discussing median, mode, and mean, the congestion of so many "m words" ends up confusing the matter and they both laugh as they slow down and start again. For a moment it seems they are understanding each other. Once Lil C grasps the concept of finding the mean of the two middle numbers to determine the median of the set, Kowanna encourages her: "Now all you have to do is figure out what the quartiles are and graph it."

"What do you *mean* find the quartiles, yo?!" Lil C pleads, despair rushing back into her voice. They break out laughing again and Kowanna explains.

Lil C proudly returns to Federal, who has a different number down for the median. "See, I tried to tell you, bro! I'm doing it right!" C beams.

A young man, who until this point has been reclining in a lounge chair with a Twin Cities hat pulled down over his eyes, making hand gestures as he listens to music, abruptly jumps up. Moments later he is perched on the edge of the chair leaning over the Mathematical Analysis of HSRA Absences paper, jotting down numbers. He continues, even as his peers get up and head off to lunch—the oft-elusive payoff of deliberate patience.

## LUNCH AND TOUCHBACK

Unlike the cliquishness that occurs at many schools, every day different collections of students gather around the rectangular lunch tables on HSRA's "blacktop," a big space that serves as a seating and eating area, as well as a performance hall. Some students have plates of meatballs, corn, and mashed potatoes provided by the school. Others have selected salad. And others still have chosen not to grab any food.

No one has brought lunch from home, but some, including Lil C, purchase snacks from the vending machines on the blacktop. C gets a bag of Flaming Hot Cheetos, carefully sliding her sleeves up her arms to avoid getting fluorescent orange marks on her white hoody.

On this particular day, Lil C sits down with Fat Ellen and Brooklynne. After a few minutes of eating and talking, Otis, the student who popped his head into TC's office earlier, comes over to their table with a sheet of paper containing the lineup for an upcoming artist showcase at the school. Known as a Pick Me Up, the showcase will occur on Friday at the end of the school day.[6]

This week's Pick Me Up is going to be a contest sponsored by the student-run record label, Another Level Entertainment. Otis has arranged for three music business professionals to attend as judges. Similar to reality shows such as American Idol or America's Best Dance Crew, the judges will not only rank the performers, they will also give them public feedback on their performances.

Otis shows Lil C her placement in the order of artists. As C studies the list, a discussion breaks out among the other students at the table about a recent talent show on the North Side.

"I made two stacks off that show," Otis states proudly.

"Cuz you didn't pay us!" C shouts. A conversation ensues about who at the talent show deserved to get paid and why.

"We all local artists," Brooklynne declares. "We're nobodies."

"Not me!" C says, jumping up from her seat. "I'm somebody! I was in the *City Pages*! I went to LA—"

"You might wanna ask TC how he really know me," Otis interjects. "I shook hands with the mayor."

"So? I shook the mayor's hand too—on TV!" Lil C is fired up. She's still standing, ready for the next attack on her character. The flurry of braggadocio continues and includes tales of having met Jay-Z, Diddy, and Bow Wow, and being down with Lil Wayne's record label, Young Money.

Across the blacktop, four students are gathered around a grand piano and a set of drums. One student is playing chords, while another lays down a drumbeat. The other two are taking turns freestyling.

Dario comes over to check in with Lil C and others about student profiles that he is putting together for Pick Me Up. Before the artist showcase each week, he presents profiles of a few students at the school to help everyone get to know more about each other. He checks information that he has on their profiles and makes sure that they are comfortable having him present the information on a slide in front of the whole school.

A voice comes booming out of the speakers situated at the sides of the stage on the blacktop: "Time for Touchback! Everybody go to Touchback!"

The source of the voice is Virgil Jackson Jr., better known as Mick Boulevard, who is dashing and dancing around the room with a wireless microphone. "Everybody go to Touchback!" He says over and over, beat-boxing in between.

A few dozen students who did not eat lunch on the blacktop roll in and find seats. Several people are involved in the production of Touchback, which serves as a midday checkpoint for connecting and communicating as a community. Uncle Phil is in the sound booth. A student in a White Sox hat is filming with a digital camera.

Mick Boulevard hands the mic to a young man with a guitar strapped to his back, who announces that there will be a freestyle cipher at the beginning of the community meeting that will occur later in the afternoon. His announcement is striking because it is the first time he has spoken out loud to anyone in the school in over a week. For the last seven days, he has been communicating entirely through gestures, facial expressions, and writing. When people spoke to him, he would just smile and put a finger over his lips. At most schools, such an exercise would guarantee suspension; at HSRA this student is working on a project about his experiments with silence.

One of Lil C's advisory mates, Miss Marzetti, announces the date by which all validations must be submitted in order for students to be eligible for the next graduation. There is a graduation every month at HSRA to accommodate students who are ready to present digital portfolios that show all of their completed validations.

Dario announces an upcoming trip to the park to celebrate Earth Day. He lists some of the activities that will be available.

"Can we have jump ropes?" a student shouts out.

"I'm not opposed to jump ropes," Dario responds, lowering the mic and turning to consult with other staff members. A few seconds later he turns back: "We'll get them."

As soon as these announcements have been made, the beat for one of Mick Boulevard's songs kicks in. He jumps on stage and starts rapping. When he's done, another beat drops. Lil C lights up. She has a verse on this song. She puts down her Cheetos and jumps up to run on stage. When she spits her verse, she goes so hard that her MP3 player flies out of her hoody.

TC is the last to speak. "You've gotta come to community meeting to get special incentive awards for testing and to hear about the prom," he stresses, before Mick Boulevard announces that Touchback is "officially over."

## PROJECT PRESENTATION

Students stream out of the blacktop toward their respective advisories for Daily Language Arts. By the time Lil C enters her advisory, students are seated in a circle. She grabs a swivel chair in the middle of the circle and spins around on it.

The bulk of today's forty-five minute Daily Language Arts block in the KDA advisory room is being used for a student to present a project she has been working on. Lil C rolls her chair over toward a projection screen as Miss Marzetti's title slide comes up: "Sex, Porn and Her Industry" it says at the top, followed below by the question: "Does Sex Sell?"

Marzetti does not need to complete any validations related to this project but decided to do the research and present it because the topic is of interest to her. She walks the group through slides such as "Reasons women join the porn industry," "Correlations between careers in porn and histories of abuse/addiction," and "Does 'sex' make a man reach for his wallet?"

At one point, she is reading a slide and gets stuck on a word. "I don't know what that word is," she announces.

"Then why'd you use it?" Kowanna asks. Her tone is not harsh and the question is not rhetorical.

"It was just something I came across in my research," Marzetti explains.

"You should have looked it up," Lil C suggests.

When Marzetti states that "Most prostitutes are drug addicts," specifically "crack heads," Kowanna presses her for the sources of her information.

Marzetti goes on to share more statistics about the pornography industry, including how much is viewed online and how much money is spent on it. She highlights statistics around child exploitation in porn, showing a clip of an Internet video of a toddler in a diaper dancing around a stripper pole. She concludes the presentation with the following warning: "Sex may sell, but you gotta remember who's watching."

Evaluation forms are passed around and all attendees, including students, advisors, the school's education director and English facilitator Paula Anderson, and a visitor, are asked to fill them out. The six questions on the form include whether the project was presented in an interesting and creative manner, and whether the presenter seemed to have a good understanding of the subject matter.

Students jot down responses indicating that they found the topic to be of high interest and appreciated Marzetti's use of media. Specific recommendations include having less information on each slide and making a bibliography available for future presentations. Kowanna collects the forms as everyone streams out of the room on the way to community meeting.

## COMMUNITY MEETING

While Touchback takes place every day after lunch and serves as a brief opportunity for announcements, community meetings occur once each week and offer a more extensive occasion for schoolwide dialogue and presentations.[7]

Mick Boulevard is on stage again. This time a dude wearing a Twins hat with fuzzy earflaps joins him. Each of them has a mic, and they start the meeting by having everyone on the blacktop recite the four values of Studio 4 out loud together: family, community, respect, and education.

One mic gets passed to TeLisa "Taz" Powell, Kowanna's younger sister, who was also a student at the school before becoming a paraprofessional. Taz requests a moment of silence for Keith Turnipseed, a staff member from the school who was murdered two years earlier. A slide pops up on a big screen behind her with a picture of Keith and the phrase "In Remembrance."

For the next several minutes, the microphone is passed around as staff and students give each other "Keith Awards." Kowanna gives a shout out to the staff members who helped get dresses for girls for the upcoming prom. A student thanks Mike for his help preparing for the Minnesota Comprehensive Assessments (MCA) math test. Another student thanks staff members Darlene Leiding and Tracy Richardson for their support and adds, "My uncle, Keith. That's why I'm still here, my uncle."

The young man with the guitar strapped to his back grabs the mic and tells everyone, "I got expelled out of my last school." Whether or not it was for being silent, his statement confirms that young people with eccentricities like his are not embraced in most schools. "We spoiled here," he continues. "I wanna give a Keith award to TC. If TC didn't exist, the school wouldn't have existed and where would I be?" He is interrupted by applause. "Also, to all the staff. These teachers don't have to be here. This is the only school I know where teachers tell you they love you. And that means something."

"Big Layne" Bellamy, the school's facilities manager, gives a shout out to everyone who took the recent statewide standardized tests, "people on their game actively pursuing their goal, everyone who comes in and is respectful"—he lists the four values of Studio 4—"if you ain't on that, you ain't part of the fo', you just sit here by our good graces. So I wanna give this award to everyone who reps it here and at home."

Beyond the occasional school assemblies where an honor roll list is read off by an administrator, most schools do not create the time and space for members of the community to celebrate each other. The Keith Awards take about five minutes each week and don't require any special preparation or materials. By catching each other doing things right and honoring the memory of a beloved member of the community, they play a powerful role in creating a familial feel among the people who populate the school each day.

Next, the student hosts invite up everyone who wants to freestyle. Five boys and one girl come to the stage. A bunch of other students stand up close to the stage as the first emcee spits hard a capella with a warm echo on his voice. He's followed by the formerly silent student, who rhymes "Buddhist" and "Jewish" in a mellower flow.

Throughout the freestyles, the student hosts regulate the vibe of the emcees and the audience. When one of the rappers drops the N-word and a graphic sexual reference, one of the hosts interjects to remind him to "keep it inexplicit." A little later, some people in the crowd boo an emcee who raps too quietly. The hosts quickly remind them, "Hey, hey, no boos! Only 'ayyys' and claps!" The audience seems to get the message as the cipher ends with applause.

Two girls get up to make an announcement about a scholarship that covers full tuition for students from low-income families. "I'm going to Harvard!" Lil C shouts. "That's a law school," another student at her table says. Playful bickering ensues.

TC steps to the mic and talks about the importance of trying hard on the standardized tests that students are being asked to take. "Every one of you transfer this message to every other one of you. Dig deep down to the basement of your heart and bring it out through the balcony of your mind. Let's knock 'em off their feet!"

He calls the name of each student who completed a recent standard- ized test. Everyone claps between names. 50 Cent's song "I Get Money" comes bumping out the speakers, the music video playing on the screen behind the stage. As students' names are called, they walk up, give TC a pound, and collect a ten-dollar bill.

There are so many mandated tests it has been hard to get students to take them all, especially because most of the tests have no bearing on students' futures and many students report having had bad experiences with tests in the past. The staff members at HSRA who correspond with the state department of education about the school's annual test results have tried a number of strategies to ensure that students take the tests.

On the one hand, HSRA's staff recognizes that the tests are not authentic assessments of the knowledge and skills students develop through HSRA's program; on the other hand, they understand that the school's ability to continue offering such a program depends on the results. One way they try to encourage students to take the tests is by offering small financial incentives donated by a friend of the school.

As the "I Get Money" sample that 50 Cent's hit borrowed from Audio Two fades out, Dario, who is DJing from the sound booth pulls up "Money" by Liza Minelli and Joel Grey. Next up is Birdman's "Money to Blow" featuring Lil Wayne. As the last students collect their cash, the community meeting turns into socializing with music in the background. Lil C goes to the vending machines with Fat Ellen. A moment later, the music is lowered.

Taz is back on the mic. "There's a paper on your tables that says 'HSRA Prom Royalty.' Fill out your nominations for king, queen, prince, and princess."

People start wiling, arguing about who deserves to be nominated. Taz asks for their attention, but side conversations have taken over. The room continues to get louder.

"Hold up!" Big Layne shouts. "Did Johnson, Henry, Arlington ever pay you to take a test?"

"Hell no!!" a student shouts.

"TC stood on this stage not twenty minutes ago and asked for your help. He tryna show you love the best way he know how." Big Layne reprimands students for acting out and implores them to improve their behavior.

Once the room has grown quiet, Taz presents a slideshow about the prom. It features pictures of past HSRA proms and information about the upcoming event.

"Girls, if you didn't already come with us for dresses and you need help finding something, come see me. Boys, come swagged out," Taz requests. "Also, if you wanna attend but can't afford it, come holla at me. And, if you don't have all the money at once, but you wanna give me five each week, Taz *will* do layaway." Free VIP tickets are available through a poster design contest and an essay writing contest, which Darryl Young, HSRA's special education facilitator, is sponsoring out of his own pocket.

In addition to the options that exist for free tickets and payment plans, the tickets are inexpensive, costing only $15 (about one quarter the amount paid by students at nearby St Louis Park High School).[8] HSRA hosts the event at the school, keeping expenses low to make tickets as affordable as possible.

All of a sudden, the speakers boom a "student of the week" anthem produced by HSRA students. "This week, instead of student of the week," S. Michelle "Miki Starr" Martin, an advisor and the school's graphics facilitator, announces there will be a "peacekeeper of the week award," which she proceeds to present.

Throughout the meeting, internal garage doors have been pulled down to separate the blacktop from the giant open space that is home to most of HSRA's advisories. The doors are raised as the community meeting's masters of ceremonies give their final farewell to the audience. "Now go read a book!"

## QUIET READING AND AFTERNOON BLOCKS

Back in the KDA advisory room, Kowanna puts out a box of books that she bought with a combination of school funds and money she raised by selling iced tea and snacks. Some students pull books out of their bags, while others pick up books that Kowanna has laid on the table. The room is rarely silent, but once things settle into a quiet murmur, Kowanna settles down at her desk with a book called *Principle-Centered Leadership* and models reading and note-taking.

Lil C reads *Blueprints*, a self-published novel about a closeted homosexual man by HSRA staff member Miki Starr Martin. After half an hour, C scoots out the door of the advisory and down the hall to the video editing room where two alumni, Jamal Aiken and the Real Young Bishop, who now works at the school as a studio facilitator, are sitting with a current student and Uncle Phil.

Lil C says, "What's up?" to everyone and then gets quickly to her agenda: She has heard that a movie called *Step Up 3* is looking for submissions for their soundtrack and she wants to send something, but she needs Bishop's help producing and engineering the song. Unfortunately, it has to be submitted this week and Bishop will not be in beyond this afternoon.

"Are there any tracks you can do without Bishop?" Phil asks.

"No," C responds matter-of-factly. And then she playfully adds, "He tells me what I'm doing wrong!"

"Maybe you could get someone to switch with you," Phil suggests, looking over the studio schedule. He comes upon the name of a student who has the studio booked for part of the afternoon but warns that "she's gonna be tough."

Lil C and Bishop move from logistics to artistics. "I have an up tempo beat," he says as he scrolls through files on the computer in front of him. Lil C spits the chorus she's been composing for the new song: "It's time to step it *UP*/Take it to the streets/I'll show you things that you can only see in 3D." She repeats it four times, on the third, Bishop starts beatboxing the kind of beat that might sound good beneath it.

They agree that they should create something new and walk down the hall to the preproduction room. It's full of students wearing headphones and composing on MIDI keyboards and computer screens so, despite the fact that someone has the main studio booked, they head over to check it out. The student on the schedule isn't there and the two quickly settle in to work.

## IN THE STUDIO

Black pen, purple grip, orange clip, gold tip. Lil C taps her colorful pen on the table. Bishop has started to program a drumbeat in ProTools. Lil C is drumming along. She does not want to write her verses until the beat is complete.

The two artists go back and forth on how the beat-in-progress fits with the hook she's written. Is it the right speed? Does it have the drive that the words convey?

While Bishop crafts the beat, C goes on a mission to find "Little Layne" Bellamy (Big Layne's son, who is also an alum-employee of the school) to see if he can engineer for her, in case she and Bishop don't have time to finish the track this afternoon.

In the hall, Lil C runs into a friend of the school and informal mentor, Susan Campion. Susan is a locally based business consultant and instructor at the Center for Business Excellence at the University of St. Thomas. The two became friendly as Susan worked closely with the students and alumni to promote the video about Haiti. Susan is at the school to meet with a recent graduate to help him on his college application. Lil C invites her to stop by the studio when she is done.

After C rejoins Bishop, several visitors pop in. Fellow alumni-turned-staff-member, Kash comes in to ask Bishop for instrumentals for a mix-tape they are working on. A student named Kurtis Greenwood comes in for his studio time. C pleads with him, "Bro, please do me a huge favor. Bishop ain't fittin' to be here for the rest of the week and we need to finish this song. Please yo, I got studio time tomorrow and Friday. Can you switch with me?"

Kurtis reluctantly agrees. Uncle Phil returns to discuss more scheduling drama, but the project has momentum now. It seems that nothing is going to get them out of the studio.

C takes off her hoody, revealing a black T-shirt with a gold Adidas logo. Bishop is creating, copying, and deleting instrument tracks at a dizzying rate.

"I don't like this," Bishop says, dragging the mouse over six tracks he has just created and hitting delete.

"You're killing me, dude," C cries out, leaning back and putting her hands on her head.

"Let's look at some of the other *Step Up* joints," Bishop says, pulling open YouTube and clicking through to the lead single from the *Step Up* 2 soundtrack, Missy Elliot's "Ching-a-Ling."

They begin watching the video. The song's beat includes sirens, whistles, and samples from the old school video game Donkey Kong.

"Missy's the truth," Bishop says with admiration.

"I wanna do a track with her one day," C agrees.

After watching the rest of the video, Bishop's got an idea: "See we gotta make it build. Make it cinematic." He clicks through dozens of menus of sounds, looking for a reverse cymbal clap, which he explains to C will "build anticipation."

As they talk about the structure of the song, he clicks and drags segments of tracks around the screen to reflect the changes they discuss. They agree that the song will come in hard with the hook at the beginning followed by a breakdown where the beat drops out.

"Then there'll be an intro like, 'introducing a lightweight champion with heavyweight skills . . . ,'" Bishop narrates, "then we let it build to a climax and you come in with all this energy. Make it epic like a movie!"

Lil C laughs, gives him dap, and grabs the brim of her fitted hat with both hands, pulling it off and back on her head, as Bishop turns up the audio monitors. The twenty-one tracks that make up the instrumental he has constructed are complex. Horns stutter, keys carry, double-time claps come in for the introduction and then disappear, and every eight bars there's a sample of a dude saying, "One, Two . . . One Two, Three, FOUR!"

"Oooh, I got another idea!" he shouts over the beat. "This is stadium music now—I want it to be stadium everything. I don't like the part for rapping. I wanna keep the beat simple while you rap, so it doesn't sound overproduced. I gotta make it more stadium."

As Bishop tweaks the beat, Lil C leans back in her chair and holds the sides of her head. "Man yo, man yo, if this happens . . . ," she trails off.

Susan enters, greets Lil C and Bishop, and takes a seat on the leather sofa from which she watches the two young artists at work and occasionally offers an opinion or a compliment. She pulls out her smart phone and updates her Twitter status: "Can't wait until @lilcthebaddest from HSRA takes over the world!! Making a big mark @17. Big talent in a small package."

Once in the vocal booth, Lil C bounces with the boom-boom-clap boom-boom-clap. "Turn off the lights yo!" she shouts to Bishop, who has positioned his chair directly between the two speakers. He has ProTools open on one screen in front of him and Facebook on the other.

"Remember, you gotta climax it," he says. "Start regular and then build up."

After C gets the hook, Bishop goes in and throws in baritone "step it ups" between the lines she has laid down. C jumps into his chair and engineers his recording. Each time he finishes one, C repositions the cursor and hits record on the next track, until Bishop has overdubbed his background vocals four times.

He comes out, turns the speakers up, and plays the beginning. Heads nod, hands motion, glances and smiles are exchanged.

Bishop goes back into the booth, tells Lil C to cue up another vocal track right at the end of the hook they just recorded and adds an "oooooowwwwweeeeee!"

On the next track, for some reason, the sound won't record. Bishop, still inside the vocal booth, offers to come out and fix the problem. A year ago, Lil C had no idea how to use ProTools—the industry standard recording software.

Now, after scrolling through a few menus, she shouts, "I got it!" A few seconds later, the beat comes cascading out of the speakers again and Bishop freestyles the introduction they had discussed: "Ladies and gentlemen . . . boys and girls of the wooooooorld! Introducing, standing at a spiffy five three and a half . . . Liiiiiiittle C!!!"

Bishop returns to the keyboard, adds distortion to the intro, and quadruples the vocal tracks he just recorded. There are already seventeen vocal tracks and Lil C hasn't laid down her verse yet.

Checking the time, Bishop announces that he has to leave. He asks Lil C if she wants him to "bounce down" the skeleton of the song so she can write to it.

"How do you think I should come at it though?" she asks.

"Like you a dancer. It's not a swagg song," Bishop warns. "Come at it like you tryna prove yourself."


## HEADING HOME

Susan offers Lil C a ride and on the way home C describes how much she's learned from Bishop: "He's taught me everything! He got me to step outta doing just one genre. Like, I made a Jerk It movement song. I sing. He's been teaching me how to engineer. And I don't do overdubs over all my lyrics now. I sound cleaner." [9]

The drive to South St. Paul only takes about twenty minutes on the highway. Lil C and Susan talk about a variety of topics, but mostly the conversation returns to music. They discuss an upcoming performance at the school and Susan tells Lil C about the CD that's playing, "Rádio Do Canibal," a compilation album featuring local and internationally known emcees over Brazilian influenced beats.[10]

The beat on track eleven slides in and locally based rapper P.O.S.'s voice bounces over it: "*Sittin,*' listenin' for a *rhythm*, tryna construct a *pattern*, pryin' apart my *habits*, dying to make it *happen* . . ."[11]

Lil C's head bops as she looks out the window at baseball diamonds and soccer fields blurring by. Little boys are taking off their cleats and climbing into minivans. It is dusk and practice is over.


## NOTES

1. Students and staff members are referred to by their first names and/or nicknames throughout this chapter, because that is how people refer to each other at the school.

2. Many people refer to HSRA as "Studio 4," because when the school was founded that was the name of the recording studio that it was centered on. Studio 4 continues to be the name of the company that provides education management and studio services to the school.

3. For an introduction to HSRA's learning areas, see chapter 1 of this book.

4. Otis's last name is omitted to protect his anonymity.

5. PSEO is an acronym for Post-Secondary Education Option, which is a program that allows high school students in Minnesota to take college courses for free.

6. The term Pick Me Up is borrowed from The Big Picture Learning school design. At Big Picture schools, Pick Me Ups do not serve as artist showcases but rather as all-school events where some type of engaging/energizing presentation occurs. For more information, see www.bigpicture.org.

7. See chapter 1 for more information about community meetings at HSRA.

8. Ben Kahn, "Prom: Good Time on a Dime," *The Echo*, http://www .slpecho.com/index.php?story=194 (June 12, 2010).

9. Jerkin' is a style of dance that started a few years ago in Los Angeles, California, and has become popular across the United States.

10. BK-One with Benzilla, *Rádio Do Canibal*, Rhymesayers, 2009, compact disc.

11. Stefon Alexander aka P.O.S., "A Day's Work," *Rádio Do Canibal*, Rhymesayers, 2009, compact disc.

# ③

# HIP-HOP LEADERSHIP

You must know failure before success
So this is the failure I must confess
I was hanging on the street trying to deal with this
Playing the games almost got dismissed . . .
From the top to the bottom, the bottom to the top
Success is where I'm headed, there ain't no doubt
Success is something we all want
But the truth is what you need to reach that point.

—David "TC" Ellis

The materialist doctrine that men are products of circumstances and upbringing, and that, therefore, changed men are products of other circumstances and changed upbringing, forgets that it is men that change circumstances and that the educator himself needs educating.

—Karl Marx and Friedrich Engels

There are five rules. . . . The first one is to wear your flyest s°°t every day. Look somebody in their eye and tell them "nope!" Be your own boss, don't take no s°°t from nobody, and make the rest of it up yourself.

—Bonz Malone

**D**avid "TC" Ellis is a great school leader. This statement is true not *despite* the academic struggles he went through as a student but *because* of them.

Conquering these challenges—in combination with a range of accomplishments—has put TC in a position from which he is able to connect with the diverse set of people that one encounters when running a high school and recording studio.[1] It has enabled him to understand the broad spectrum of experiences that comprise the realities for students and families at the High School for Recording Arts (HSRA).

TC has built the school to reflect and make room for all of the talents and tragedies students bring through the door each day. From fistfights to spotlights to airplane flights, the events in TC's life and the way he has handled them have played a central role in the development of HSRA.

This chapter shares stories that illustrate TC's experiences before, during, and after starting the school. These tales reveal the genesis of the school's unique program and highlight TC's unorthodox brand of leadership.

Some of the following stories have become legends that have been passed down like a game of telephone over the past decade in the HSRA community. Details may have, over time, been rewritten or exaggerated. This is not to suggest the stories are untrue, but rather to make the point that their historical veracity is not paramount. In the long tradition of parables that are passed down to communicate morals or lessons to live by, what is most important about these stories is the values that they communicate to students, staff, and visitors of the school.

## FLIP ABILITY

People actually began calling me "TC" before I started rapping. That was back when I was hustling. We grew up in St. Paul, and in the Twin Cities, if you're from Minneapolis or St. Paul, it's like a territorial beef. Still today kids get killed behind that. It isn't as much of a thing for girls to cross the line; it's mostly the guys that are beefin'.

My sister had a girlfriend who lived over in North Minneapolis and one summer they came over to our house in St. Paul for a picnic and the girlfriend's younger sister came with her. I liked the younger sister, so I ended up venturing over to Minneapolis to court her. I knew it was dangerous, but you know what a woman can do to you.

So I was over there kickin' it and I ended up at the McDonald's by her house. All these cats are comin' in there, y'know, like the real thugs, the tough dudes from the neighborhood and they're questioning who I am and where I'm from. So I hear 'em talking and they're like, "That dude's from St. Paul," "Ain't that cat from St. Paul?" And one of the dudes comes up to me and says, "Man, ain't you from St. Paul?"

And I say, "No."

So he says, "Well, where you from then?"

". . . I'm from the Twin Cities."

And he stands there for a minute and then he's like, "Oh, you 'TC,' right? You 'TC,'" and he slaps my hand.

From then on, they called me TC over North and I had a visa whereby I could handle business over there. So I became the person who could go back and forth between the Twin Cities without havin' a problem. That opened up my worth on the street, cuz I could go to Minneapolis without fear and hustle over there or if somebody had business from Minneapolis they wanted to take care of in St. Paul, I could handle that too.

This is the story of how David "TC" Ellis got his name. If not for his quick wit and ingenuity, the incident in the North Minneapolis McDonald's would likely have led to a beat down; instead, it became an urban vision quest that ended up providing TC with a moniker that signifies his ability to move across boundaries—in this case, between cities—that for many are impassable.

The same ability to think on his feet when it came to names would come in handy years later when TC was building the studio that eventually became HSRA. In the mid-nineties, TC was trying to assemble equipment but was running into challenges finding the funds for everything required to make it a top-notch recording studio.

Meanwhile, a younger "nephew-cousin" of his had a gangsta rap crew and they had built an impressive studio off of street hustle money. Their crew had recorded some songs and had a good underground buzz around the Twin Cities. When their album was complete, they decided they wanted to have a huge release party.

TC tried to convince them to have smaller shows first and build up to something big, but they got ahead of themselves and planned a show at one of the largest clubs in town. The show was a disaster—they got on stage way late, the sound was terrible, and a huge fight broke out. In that one night, the group combusted.

Soon after, the nephew-cousin was losing his studio space and he approached TC about providing a home for the soon-to-be orphaned equipment. TC was amped at the prospect of his studio being better amped. But there was a catch: The nephew-cousin did not want to let his crew's legacy die. The studio would have to take on the name of their gangsta rap group, "Down 4 Dirt."

"I was like, 'Well, y'know, I'm not down with no 'Down 4 Dirt' shit," TC recalls. "He was like, 'Ain't there no way we can keep the "4" alive?' So I was like, 'If we can keep the equipment, we can keep the '4' alive. . . . We'll make it 'Studio 4.'

This compromise that TC crafted made it possible for him to assemble a high-quality recording studio without carrying on the negative legacy of his nephew-cousin's crew. All was good, until a few years later, when HSRA received its approval as a charter school. The event garnered local media attention and a newspaper reporter asked TC what the "4" in Studio 4 represented.

"In my head, I was like, 'Damn, it came from Down 4 Dirt,' but that was when I got blessed," TC recollects. "Y'know, it just came off the top. I was like, 'Well, that's family, respect, community, and education.'"

Surely there can be some risk and lost opportunities that come with such spontaneity. Many schools or organizations would have had a series of meetings to identify the core values of their community. Surveys would have gone out, results would have been measured and discussed, decision-making methods would have been agreed upon. In this way, they would have ensured a thorough selection process, with broad buy-in from everyone involved.

But TC didn't have time for a series of meetings. He was taking Down 4 Dirt equipment and repurposing it for something positive. At that moment, a newspaper reporter had put him on the spot and he needed a socially acceptable answer for the name of the company. He looked into his heart, pulled on the improvisational wordplay skills that he had honed as a rapper, and trusted that what came out would be right. The article was glowing and the school continued growing.

TC has never regretted making such an important decision in the spur of the moment. "It was really the perfect building block we needed at the time," he says. The staff and students instantly took to it; and to this day, family, respect, community, and education stand strong as the pillars of the HSRA community.

"I realize now that that spontaneous style was part of the school's essence. The experimentation is very important to the viability and attraction of the school. If the intent is good and the work is good. . . . Let some things come about as they may."

Beyond the name, when it came to building the recording studio that eventually became HSRA, TC had to be resourceful. He did not have a budget, had never written a grant, and had minimal formal business experience. So he went to the richest guy he knew, Wolfie.

Wolfie was a hoodstar. He drove a souped-up Cadillac Coupe de Ville and tossed around money. But behind the flashy style, Wolfie was an extremely hard worker with a methodical attention for detail. "He was a known genius in the street for his creative hustles," TC recalls. "Everyone's passionate about something. . . . Wolfie had a paper fetish."

Wolfie loved the idea of being a part of a recording studio and began employing the work ethic and sensibilities he had honed in the street to help make the studio a reality. Wolfie's partners would give him a hard time about pouring his time and money into his newfound passion. They'd come at him like, "You're takin' a bath on that studio shit" and he'd be like, "If you wanna get cleaned up, you gotta take a bath." Being part of the studio team was Wolfie's way of moving away from street economics and into building a positive institution.

Once the studio was built, TC found ways to continue to connect Wolfie with constructive work. "The same intelligence he was known for in the street came in handy starting a school. Wolfie was great with paperwork, like organizing binder books of education procedures and studying compliance regulations from the district. He was obsessed with playing everything strictly by the book. He'd be like, 'Look, you need to show the fire department this right here.' He was all into regulatory shit."

Wolfie also had such a thorough reputation in the street that, until leukemia claimed his life, his presence at the school rendered discipline issues virtually nonexistent. "If there was a problem, there wasn't no one in the game he couldn't reach out to and get it resolved," TC explains. "Wolfie'd come in like, 'What the fuck are you doing?' And that was the end of it. He just was not challenged."

When TC decided to start a school, he could have cut off his street affiliations. Instead he flipped those relationships into resources that helped create and run the school.

Without his nephew-cousin's equipment and Wolfie's help, TC couldn't have built the school in the literal brick-and-mortar sense. Without Wolfie's presence and sensibilities, he would not have been as successful at appealing to or working effectively with kids from the 'hood. Without his own ingenuity, he wouldn't have been able to flip Down 4 Dirt to the four pillars of Studio 4 or Wolfie's street skills and reputation into assets for a high school.

## RELENTLESS HUSTLE

I was very entrepreneurial when I was in elementary school. I was into shining shoes. I had built me a shoeshine box and I would go up and down the busy street by my house, which was University Avenue, and I would literally go into bars and give guys a shine and they'd flip me a buck or two. I remember being seven or eight years old with nine or ten bucks in my pocket.

From there I advanced to selling candy. That was a big thing. We would go to this discount store, and we could buy these glossy, shiny boxes of candy, where they'd cost like a quarter a box, but we could sell 'em for a buck. So we'd buy a case of them for like four bucks and go out and sell 'em all for a dollar a box. That didn't include the other people who were just like, "I don't want no candy, but here's a dollar." We'd tell 'em we were selling candy for school or Boys Club or sum'n like that, but we were hustling. I liked that. I saw that it worked.

What do a shoe-shiner, a candy salesman, a drug dealer, an airplane pilot, a special events manager for the *Saint Paul Pioneer Press* newspaper, a juvenile corrections worker, a brakeman for the Canadian Pacific Railroad, an actor, and a signed rapper, ghostwriter, and producer all have in common?

They are all jobs TC held in the first thirty-five years of his life. The world around TC was flowing quickly. To stay afloat, he had to stay making moves. There was a period when he got pulled under by the current, struggling with a cocaine addiction, but even his path back to sobriety required determined resilience.

"The third time through rehab I got it. It was a battle for the life, believe that. It took everything in me to finally get it." Despite all of the pain and temptation, TC buckled down and studied the twelve steps. Redemption and confession were a part of the program. These concepts inspired him to riff off of his moniker and, out of the lowest moment in his life, write a rap that would change everything, launching him to higher heights than he could imagine:

> True Confessions if you listen close you about to learn a lesson
> You must know failure before success
> So this is the failure I must confess
> I was hanging on the street trying to deal with this
> Playing the games almost got dismissed
> Cocaine was the thing that I took on
> And nowhere was the place that I was going
> Now I must tell the truth I cannot lie
> I was headed for the kill, steal, destroy and die
> From the top to the bottom, the bottom to the top
> Success is where I'm headed there ain't no doubt
> Success is something that we all want
> But the truth is what you need to reach that point
> The truth is something you can't deny
> Your only defense is to tell a lie
> I had to give this message the stone cold truth
> I hope there's something in it that's there for you
> Like I said before and I'ma tell you again
> Success is something that's deep within
> So remember the truth you can't go wrong
> The flesh is weak but the spirit is strong
> I had to do this rap and I know it's right
> Cuz I did it in the name of Jesus Christ
> It's the True Confession
> Check it out for your protection

The True Confession
You listen close you might make a connection[2]

TC refers to "True Confessions" as "the rap that broke me free." Soon after he finished writing it, he got out of treatment and began what has now been over twenty years of sobriety.

Immediately after completing rehab, TC began tirelessly pursuing entry to the recording industry. The most obvious path was to get down with Prince and the Revolution. The superstar Prince grew up in the Twin Cities at the same time as TC. TC's sister had sung in a group with Prince and TC was friends with his bodyguards. But there was a problem: Prince didn't like rap.

"Every time I'd see him, I'd confront him and ask him how he could not like rap. I didn't believe him. You're a virtuoso, how can you not like rap?" TC approached Prince on multiple occasions and requested his help getting into the music business. "His answer was consistently, 'No,' and he was getting irritated with me."

But TC could not be deterred. When Prince started working on the soundtrack for *Batman*, his guitar player, who was a friend of TC's, told TC information about the movie that he was learning from watching the dailies.

"I convinced [the guitar player] to do the music for me and I did a rap called the 'Bat Rap.' I put everything he told me was gonna be in the movie in the song and put it out before the movie came out. It was kind of expensive to get records pressed up, but I hustled. I had backers in the community and lots of people in the family pitched in because I was crazy about it. I was obsessed with making these rap records. I'd just do it any way I could get it done."

While recording the "Bat Rap," TC told Prince's guitar player about his early relationship with Prince: "Back in the day before Prince had all the bodyguards, I took up for him. One time a guy in the club who had a baby with a girl that Prince was messing with came at him pointing his finger tryna get in his ass. I got in his way and I had a lil rep in the neighborhood because I boxed Golden Gloves, so dude backed off and Prince was thankful."

The guitar player said, "Remind him, remind Prince of that!"

The next time TC saw Prince, he did.

"What, do I owe you for that?" Prince asked him, reaching for money.

"I told him, 'Nah, why don't you open the door and let me get it myself?' And he just said, 'That was then, this is now' and did his little strut away from me."

But when Prince's label Warner Brothers heard the Bat Rap, they were interested and asked Prince about it. Finally TC got the call, "Hey T, why don't you get your stuff and bring it out to Paisley Park?" They started cutting the album, *True Confessions*, right then.

Not only did Prince help TC negotiate a recording contract with Warner Brothers, take him on tour, and hook him up with George Clinton, Mavis Staples, Patti Labelle, and Tevin Campbell, but TC's persistent pursuit made such an impression on Prince that he wrote a part for TC in his next film, *Graffiti Bridge*. The role portrayed a character named TC chasing Prince around constantly asking to rap. At the end, TC gets his chance to perform with the New Power Generation. In the movie, this progression takes place over the course of a week; in real life, creating that opportunity took several years of relentless hustle.

## CONFIDENT COLLABORATION

I had no plan on going to the Million Man March at all. I kinda got roped into it by my old mentor, Bobby Hickman. I was trying not to go, but Bobby just told me, "I'm gonna come pick you up tomorrow."

When we got to DC it was so incredible, we went to the hotel and decided not to even stay there. We went right to the National Mall and camped out. I remember in the morning when I woke up and the sun was coming up and there was just a sea of people coming in like water flowing into a lake.

We weren't probably a hundred feet away from where Farrakhan and different people were coming to speak. Farrakhan had a strong message to us to go back to our communities and do something that was healing, something that was going to be positive and supportive of our community and people in general. He really kept it all human. It wasn't all about race and being black, it was more about being a positive human being and doing something positive in whatever community you were in.

At that time, I was running a recording studio and all these kids kept hanging around my studio during the day. I'd tell them to go to school, but they'd tell me how school was wack, and that what they wanted to do was learn how to make money off making music. They wanted to learn, but just didn't have the right avenues. The march was a confirmation of what I was already thinking in my mind about what I needed to do.

The whole van ride back to St. Paul I was talking about how I wanted to start a school. Bobby kept checking me, "What you're trying to do ain't easy, it's a lot of work."

I respected Bobby and I was listening to him, but I was just blissed out. Sometimes I believe ignorance is bliss, because, honestly, if I woulda known about all the compliance issues and everything that goes along with operating a school, I probably wouldn'ta been able to do what I did. Knowing what I know now, I probably never would have started HSRA. But at that time Bobby couldn't talk me out of it. I listened to him, but I had an instinct that had been following me and I had to follow it.

Standing on the National Mall, listening to Farrakhan and looking out at the sea of Black men who had come together for the Million Man March, TC had decided to start a school for young people who shared his passion for music and his beefs with the traditional school system. He was positive that the school he envisioned should exist. He knew that he was the right person to found it, but he was also aware of his own limitations. He was proud of his vision, yet did not have too much pride to accept help.

TC had experienced the power of collaboration before he decided to start a school. Like many emcees, he was cocky and competitive, but he was also smart enough to take advice and assistance. George Clinton coached him on his cadence and delivery. Clinton's son, Treylewd, wrote rhymes for TC's album. TC was confident enough in himself not to reject these offerings of support the way many rappers do.

His openness for collaboration served TC as he entered the world of school start-up and administration. He had strong instincts when it came to what type of environment and educational experiences students needed. But when it came to following regulations, it was Wolfie who had dexterity with documents and an eye for detail.

TC also began enlisting others who could strengthen his vision and help transform it into reality. He reached out to past mentors, such as Bobby Hickman, who had run youth programs. He also reconnected with a teacher and the principal from the St. Paul Open School, the alternative high school from which he had graduated twenty years earlier.

The teacher, Joe Nathan, had become a national expert on school reform and was able to advise him and help put academic language to the ideas TC had about how he wanted to structure the school. The principal from St. Paul Open School, Dr. Wayne Jennings, had become the principal of another school nearby and was thrilled to see an old student interested in continuing the legacy of providing alternatives for students who rejected or were rejected by the mainstream.

Dr. Jennings offered to make TC's studio a satellite program from his school. The satellite status helped channel funding to TC's program, which allowed him to hire his first teacher.

While providing some dollars was important, Dr. Jennings also offered TC his perspective from fifty years in the education game. He pulled on his experience in schools and his educational research—he has hundreds of articles published to help TC design the academic program for HSRA. Dr. Jennings's encyclopedic knowledge of educational practices presented TC with the perfect catalog of educational models from which to select and spin a unique blend of samples, creating a fresh mix designed specifically for HSRA's students.

Soon the two men began writing the charter application that would eventually incorporate the High School for Recording Arts as its own institution. At that point, Dr. Jennings began serving as superintendent of HSRA and as chair of the school's board. In these capacities, he has made it his mission to help protect HSRA from district personnel, state-level bureaucrats, foundation program officers, and teachers who are set in their ways, all of whom have tried to force the school to take on a more traditional academic program.

Dr. Jennings's status as an education OG has made it possible for him to have TC's back in these battles. If Wolfie brought street cred to the school, Dr. Jennings brought ed cred.

As HSRA grew, TC encountered other people who could help develop the school. Paula Anderson was an English teacher and an academic coordinator at an alternative learning program in the area.[3] TC met her at an Art Crawl in downtown St. Paul, and in talking with her about his vision for the school, he found that she had experience operationalizing some of the ideas he hoped to implement.

TC pursued Paula as relentlessly as he had Prince: Every time they saw each other, he asked her to work at HSRA. At first she refused, so he would pay her $50 to come by and talk to his staff about the idea of competency-based graduation plans, which had become an area of expertise for Paula through her position at the alternative learning program.

As Paula spent time at the school through her sporadic visits, she came to see it as a place that not only permitted but fostered innovation, a school where there was no box to have to think outside of.

Having hosted a punk rock radio show in college, Paula wasn't a hip-hop head, but she understood the power of music. As she grew to appreciate what a unique environment HSRA was, the Prince treatment prevailed and Paula came to work at HSRA as the academic director. With Joe Nathan and Dr. Jennings as advisors, and Paula on site, TC had crossed the "t" and dotted the "i" in "education."

When it came to the business aspects of running the studio and school, such as selecting a location, soliciting donations, or negotiating contracts, TC had a lot of confidence. Perhaps too much. His style sometimes came across as brash and aggressive.

He would show up to meetings and speak from his heart, but some people could not hear his message through his street vernacular, or else they would be put off by his baggy attire. Rather than pretend to be someone he was not, TC acknowledged his need for a CL Smooth to his Pete Rock. As long as someone had on a suit and tie, he could keep wearing his hoody and gold chain.

Tony Simmons was the perfect candidate. Tony was an entertainment lawyer TC had met through the music business. TC and Tony had hit it off at a music conference on the East Coast, but Tony had family in Minnesota, so whenever he'd come out, TC would get him to come by the school and give seminars on the business of music.

When it came time for the school's charter to be reviewed, TC was confident he knew what needed to be said. But he asked Tony to come out and help with how to say it. "I knew I was gonna offend someone and I wanted a smooth lawyer rolling with me."

"Tony is like a brother." TC describes Tony as "an extreme of another side of me. He's like the preppy, pretty boy, real smart and refined, educated type. He's not rough around the edges and I admire that."

The relationship struck a perfect balance, as Tony held an equal level of respect for TC's style and quickly fell in love with the philosophy of the school.

HSRA never would have come into existence if it weren't for the absolute conviction and clarity TC felt coming out of the Million Man March. But it also wouldn't have happened if he had not been willing to reach out to and learn from his old high school principal, a white woman who'd hosted a punk rock radio show in college, and a pretty-boy lawyer from New York City.

TC relies on this team to combine all of their skills and strengths in moments when the school comes under attack. But in other instances when he has seen a need to flip the script and do something that hasn't been done before, he has had to maintain his conviction, even when his team did not see eye to eye with him. This occurred when TC was transitioning from running a for-profit recording studio to running an educational program. He wanted to continue running the studio as a for-profit company and have the school contract the studio to provide programming.

"It was kinda crazy because initially Tony, who's an attorney, my ex-wife, who's an attorney, and another guy who was the business manager told me I couldn't do that," TC recalls. "They all told me, 'It's a conflict of interest. Make up your mind, either you wanna be a for-profit company or you're gonna be a nonprofit, and really you've gotta be a nonprofit because you want to start a school.'"

But TC refused to file the papers that would dissolve the for-profit business and incorporate it as a nonprofit organization. Call it Hip Hop Genius, a premonition, or intuition, but a few weeks later, Tony came across an article in the *New York Times* about an emerging trend of for-profits and nonprofits contracting with each other. This precedent convinced the naysayers. They prepared the paperwork, and TC got his way.

"That was something I had learned from working with Prince," TC reflects. "I wanted to stand my ground. I didn't wanna give up the autonomy of having my own company."

Having a privately held business own and operate the recording studio within the school allows for a type of flexibility unparalleled in other schools. For instance, students can record uncensored music after hours, without it having been made on equipment owned by the school district. On the other hand, the school's nonprofit status saves taxes and enables them to apply for grants and receive donations.

TC is glad he stuck to his vision, "What we're doing is really a hybrid and it gives us an opportunity to accomplish things more efficiently."

TC likens the lessons he has learned from starting the school to the skills that students will need to be able to succeed: Always be confident. Always collaborate. Get in peoples' face and don't back down, but don't be a knucklehead either. Do it with sensitivity and style. If you're passionate about a dream, think outside the box about how to bring it into reality.

"Sometimes we gotta remember with young people to not always educate them to the reality of everything that they're trying to do, because when you do that, you make the dream impossible," TC explains. "Sometimes when they don't know all the limitations, it gives them the power to do what they want to do. All they see is the goal and they don't have enough sense not to try it. They go for it, and they make it, and that's what happened to me."

## STREET CREDIBILITY

We had this one student whose father was a straight up, from the street, old school, break-it-down, hardcore pimp. He didn't have no wide-rimmed hat, but his mannerisms and his vocabulary was all the way pimp-ish: "Sit yo ass down, bitch. Don't get outta pocket. I'm tryna handle my business." He talked to his daughter and her mother in that manner.

One day this father showed up at the school, and he was upset because a young man who also went to the school had been over to his house while he was out of town. His daughter had actually invited the young man over and I guess they had sex or whatever, and the father found out about it and wanted to do something about it. So he came to the school to find the kid.

Two staff members had to pull him down off a table in the cafeteria area. He was up there shouting, "Where's this little muthafucka at?"

They brought him to my office, and he was snapping out. I happened to see a tattoo he had on his arm, and it was an old school gang tattoo I recognized because I had been in treatment with one of the founders of that gang. And that dude was tryna turn his life around as I was, but he was an old school OG, and still had his credibility.

So I asked the girl's father, "You know Martez?"

And he said, "You talking 'bout my son?"

I said, "Your son?"

And dude was like, "Yeah, my son's name's Martez."

So I said, "No, I mean Martez, the dude that founded the gang that you got on your tattoo."

And he said, "That's who my son's named after, of course, I know him."

He was still heated and talking about harming this young man, so I called my boy, Martez, and got him to talk to this dude. Martez squashed the whole situation real nice.

As a school leader, when it comes to dealing with gangs, it pays not to throw out the baby with the quarter water. TC's association with Martez did not mean that he endorsed Martez's gang activities. But it did mean that Martez respected him and when he needed Martez's help, TC could reach out to him.

At another school, a similar situation with an angry father could have gone a completely different way. It could have ended in violence right then and there. Or it could have led to the police being called in, which would have eroded trust and would likely have meant the girl withdrawing from the school. Instead, TC dealt with the parent on terms that were familiar to him and everyone wound up safe and feeling respected.

After that incident, TC made a point of developing relationships with the local leaders of other gangs so that everyone would understand that the school was a neutral zone for young people.

"I felt like, until I reached out and got the leaders on board, we could call the school a 'safe space,' but it wasn't truly safe," TC explains. So he connected with the United for Peace Gang Truce that was going on and let them know about the opportunity he was trying to provide for young people.

"A lot of these cats who are in gangs, or have been in gangs, are trying to do something to make their lives better, and they like to see something like what I'm doing. Once they understood what I was doing, they made it known to their kids that the school was neutral turf. Then the school was truly a sanctuary for kids."

Beyond being able to reach out to gang leaders when there are problems with students, TC also knows many students' families. "A lot of them are descendants of friends, community icons, or even distant family of mine," TC explains. "So once I get the scoop on a young person, I can usually dig around and get in touch with someone who cares about their life. 'Let me call his mother,' or . . . 'You know who takes care of him, his godfather!' And then this kid realizes, 'Damn, this cat knows my family,' and then he looks at it from a whole different way."

Connecting with students' families provides TC insight as to what is going on in students' lives and how best to reach them and work with them. And it demonstrates to students that he has credibility in their world outside of the school.

In instances where people misunderstand and think that HSRA is a regular school and can be accorded the same low level of respect that they feel toward other institutions, there is a large web of students, staff, alumni, and friends to correct that perception.

Once during a school graduation, while everyone was in the performance space at the back of the school, someone stole two of the school's three MIDI Production Centers (MPCs), which at the time were the centerpieces of the recording studio. The absence of the equipment delayed a lot of students' projects, so everybody in the school community knew that the studio was in need of some MPCs.

"One day I got a call from a student who had graduated, Shotty Boo, saying 'I heard you're looking for some MPCs.'" When TC relayed that the school's MPCs had been stolen, Shotty said, "Hell no! I'll call you right back." When he called back he said, "I think this is them." So they set up a meeting in the parking lot of a restaurant.

TC and Shotty Boo recognized the thieves as soon as they pulled up, because they had at one point been students at the school. As soon as they opened the trunk, TC pulled his truck up behind them.

"Shotty is like 300 pounds and he's all mad, like, 'How a muthafucka gonna steal some shit out the school?!' Before I could even stop him, he cold-cocked one of them. After that the other one froze up. We took the MPCs back and Shotty threw their keys over a building."

The school had their workstations back. But the more important outcome was the message that the recovery of the equipment sent. As TC put it, "Mufuckas on the street were like, 'Damn, it's hard to steal something from Studio 4 and not get found out.'"

This message has been reiterated periodically over the years. There are always new students who don't fully understand that even though it is called a school, HSRA has a different position in the community than Central, Highland Park, Como, or any other school in the area. TC has to reinforce his personal reputation and credibility as well.

Recently, Kowanna Powell Anderson, an HSRA advisor and alumna, was teasing TC, telling him he's gotten soft. "You didn't usedta take anything like that from students," she said, referring to a student who had been a bit disrespectful toward him at a community meeting.

"I'm not fighting any more students," TC replied. "If you fight 'em, you end up hiring 'em. Every student I've beefed with has ended up working here. We ain't got enough positions for me to fight any more students."

In the early days of HSRA, a young man named Codie Wilson moved from Gary, Indiana, to attend the school. Codie came from a tough background—he had witnessed and experienced gruesome abuse within his immediate family and had reacted by hurting others. By the time he was of high school age, he was rolling with gangsters and had been incarcerated several times. Throughout a three-year bid, he did not receive a single visitor.

Codie's brother had moved from Gary to St. Paul and told Codie about a new school starting in the Twin Cities that was offering young people the opportunity to record music. This appealed to Codie. He convinced his probation officer that this was a chance for him to turn his life around and he spent all his money on a bus ticket to St. Paul.

Codie quickly became one of the most dedicated students at HSRA, highly appreciative of the opportunity to get in the studio, record music, and learn about the entertainment industry. When some outsiders entered the studio and were threatening the safety of students, including Codie, he knocked one of them out.

Sometimes his tough demeanor created problems internally. At one point, he was so focused on a recording project, he had stopped working on his academic projects and had taken over the recording studio. Other students approached TC and complained that Codie was dominating the equipment and not allowing them to work on their projects.

When TC approached Codie, the interaction became volatile. TC felt that Codie was being disrespectful and asked him to leave for the day. But Codie, who had been consistently disappointed by male role models in his life, took TC's command to leave as a permanent banishment.

Hurt, on his way out, Codie threatened that when he saw TC in the street he was going to beat him up.

Months later, TC ran into Codie at a gas station. Sure enough, Codie approached and swung on him. TC, who fought Golden Gloves as a teenager, exchanged jabs with Codie.

Who was getting the best of whom can only be answered by those who were there, but when the police arrived, the two men hopped in TC's car together and drove around the block. While in the car, Codie told TC that next time he ran into him, he would "put some lead" in him.

TC responded, "Look, last time you told me when we saw each other you were gonna fight me and you did. So I'm taking you seriously when you say you're gonna shoot me. So you know what that means, when you see me we're gonna have to see who can shoot the best."

Most school leaders would probably have permanently banned Codie from the school and called the police. TC did go to the police. But first he went home and got his pistol, for which he had a permit. Then he went down to the police station, let them know his life had been threatened, and that he was going to be carrying his gun in self-defense. This was written up in a Protection Order. He drove over to Codie's house and showed Codie's brother the paperwork and the gun, and let him know he would be ready if he saw Codie.

Soon after, Codie moved to Las Vegas and remained there for the next few years.

While Codie was in Las Vegas, he would call HSRA and ask people what was going on at the school and with TC, in particular. The week before Wolfie died, Codie talked to him. He told Codie, "I ain't got long and I need you to go talk to T. You need to be back in school. You need to go." Eventually Codie followed through on Wolfie's appeal and returned to the Twin Cities and got together with TC. The two spoke for several hours.

Codie reenrolled at the school and graduated. He now works at the school as a security guard and dedicated utility player, hosting weekly performance showcases, and helping on any projects that come his way. His presence as a staff member demonstrates to students that HSRA embraces street dudes as long as they're on a positive path.

Codie's journey through the school is not only an illustration of TC and HSRA's street credibility. Codie is the next generation. TC has made starting schools cool for guys from the 'hood.

"A lot of kids think if you go to your block with some education or some success, people are gonna be like, 'Nigga, this the 'hood.' *No.* The 'hood wants that." Codie spoke at Hamline University as a part of a presentation about HSRA. "When I came back and pulled out the book from [the presentation], they was *happy.*"

Codie used to want to be the toughest gangster on the street. Now he sees education as the real hustle. "It's easy to be street," Codie reflects "Working to get you to understand something, that's hard."

Codie's dream is to start a school like HSRA in his hometown of Gary, where he says it is desperately needed. "Man, if I can do a school like this in Indiana, you know how many kids'll get diplomas? You know how much music will get made? Do you have any idea how many lives will be saved?"

Like Joe Nathan and Dr. Jennings did for TC, the leaders of HSRA will support Codie in carrying on the legacy of alternative educational innovations. There will inevitably be times when they will try to convince him to pace himself and move no more than a few steps at a time. And there will be times he'll have to look them in the eyes, tell them, "Nope," and then make the rest of it up himself. But as long as he keeps innovating, hustles hard, balances confidence and collaboration, and respects the brilliance of the students he is seeking to serve, Hip Hop Genius will continue to thrive.

## NOTES

1. School staff members and students are referred to by their first names and/or nicknames throughout this chapter because that is how people refer to each other at the school.

2. David Ellis, "True Confessions," *True Confessions*, Warner Brothers, 1991, compact disc.

3. Alternative learning programs, commonly referred to as area learning centers in St. Paul, offer alternative teaching methods and flexible hours in nontraditional learning environments.

# ④

# SOCIETY'S SUCKER PUNCH

The schools ain't teachin' us nothin'. . . but how to be slaves and hard workers for white people to build up they shit, make they businesses successful, while it's exploitin' us, knowhatimsayin? And they ain't teachin' us nothin' related to solvin' our own problems . . . ain't teachin' us how to stop the police from murdering us and brutalizing us . . . how to get our rent paid. They ain't teachin' our families how to interact better with each other. . . . That's why my niggas got a problem with this shit . . . cuz it don't relate. . . . And I love education, knowhatimsayin? But if education ain't elevatin' me, then . . . it ain't takin' me where I need to go, on some bullshit, then fuck education.

—Dead Prez

Urban school reform rhetoric has missed the mark. It has presumed that urban schools are broken. Urban schools are not broken; they are doing exactly what they are designed to do. This argument is not meant to excuse the academic failure in many urban schools. Instead, it is meant to shake up and radicalize the business-as-usual approach to improving urban schools by shifting the blame from the victims of an unjust system onto the fiscal, political, and ideological policies that deliberately undercut and demean urban schools.

—Jeffrey M. R. Duncan-Andrade and Ernest Morrell

Unless we change the purpose of schooling from a focus on decontextualized academic learning to the explicit teaching of the knowledge and skills needed to solve complex, undefined, and value-laden problems collaboratively in a continually changing world, we will fall short of the stated goal . . . to prepare all students for leadership and success in the global economy and society.

—Rona Wilensky

The same societal problems that make the High School for Recording Arts (HSRA) a deeply valued sanctuary for young people in the Twin Cities and a model of interest to educators near and far also threaten its existence. Institutional racism and classism, lack of financial resources, and a need to prepare for a rapidly changing world leave many young people desperate for respect, safety, and support. Schools like HSRA can meet these needs, but such schools are not exempt from the very same systems of oppression.

To understand the scenarios under which David "TC" Ellis started HSRA and has had to hustle to maintain it over the past twelve years, and the environmental factors that young leaders like Codie Wilson will face as they attempt to start similar programs, it is necessary to look at the fiscally, politically, and ideologically unjust policies and practices referred to in the epigraphs above.

Although by no means an exhaustive treatment of the ways in which society is stacked against young people of color, poor young people, and those in urban environments, this chapter gives a snapshot of the context in which HSRA exists. Urban public schools are hemorrhaging students and providing questionable preparation to many of those who remain.

Outlining these problems brings the significance of HSRA's work and the notion of Hip Hop Genius into sharp relief. It also sets the stage for presenting some of the challenges that HSRA has faced in recent years. The details of these obstacles are specific to HSRA, but they exemplify the barriers that proponents of Hip Hop Genius will inevitably run up against given the current climate around education in this country and society's seemingly timeless resistance to changes that benefit poor young people of color.

## SYSTEMIC SHORTS

Excessive policing, overincarceration, and inequalities in access to health care, housing, transportation, and employment opportunities have immediate life-and-death consequences for poor children and children of color. The flaws of the education system substantially reduce the chances of any significant transformation of these dynamics. By denying young people access to the tools to analyze and alter the situations they are in, the status quo is maintained.

The alarming rate at which students are leaving high schools across this nation is a powerful indication of how severely our education system is falling short of its responsibility to prepare all young people for life beyond school. For every three high school students who graduate, one of their peers will not. [1] On average, one student will drop out of school every twenty-six seconds. [2]

As everyone who studies education knows, the statistics become even starker when race, class, gender, sexual orientation, and population density are factored into the equation. While nationally 71 percent of students who begin high school end up graduating four years later, the percentage is dramatically lower for black, Latino, and Native American students.

According to Education Week's "Diplomas Count 2008" report, which calculated data from 2005 enrollment and graduation rates, only 55 percent of black students graduated within four years of entering high school. For Latino students, the number was slightly better, at 58 percent. And for Native American students, it was the lowest, at 51 percent. [3]

When it comes to socioeconomic status, the less money people have, the less likely they are to graduate. The Urban Institute's Education Policy Center presented "A Statistical Portrait of Public High School Graduation," which included telling statistics regarding the impact of class on high school graduation. Holding other factors constant, for every 10 percent increase in the number of free and reduced lunch recipients in a district—an indicator of poverty—the graduation rate dropped by 3.8 percent. [4]

The same report found that overall males graduate at a rate 8 percent lower than their female peers. [5] And although it is difficult to find exact statistics on the graduation rates of lesbian, gay, bisexual, and transgender young people, it is estimated that almost a third leave high school without a diploma.[6]

The Urban Institute's Education Policy Center's "Statistical Portrait" shows that students in urban school districts are less likely to graduate than students in other districts. During the time period from which the report compiled data, suburban schools had a 73 percent graduation rate, while schools in "central cities" had a 58 percent graduation rate.[7]

So, black, Latino, and Native American students are less likely to graduate than white or Asian students. And poor students are less likely to graduate than middle-class or wealthy students. And this pattern continues for male students; lesbian, gay, bisexual, and transgender students; and urban students. The inequities are glaring, but *why* are so few students graduating in general?

If the number of students who were not completing high school was much smaller, perhaps an argument could be made that these students just weren't trying hard enough. But *nearly a third of all high school students are not completing high school in four years.*

When the situation is so bad that, en masse, young people are unable or unwilling to finish, it is clear that either the system itself is broken or it was never designed to work for all students in the first place. Either way, for anyone concerned about the future of this country, the numbers cited above signal an urgent call for dramatic changes to our education system.

A major part of the reason that students stop attending school is that what is occurring in their classrooms bears no relevance to their lives. One out of two high school students surveyed in a recent study by the National Research Center for Career and Technical Education reported being bored in school *every day*. One of the top two reasons they cited for their boredom was that they did not feel the material they were studying was relevant to their lives.[8]

But the disconnect between students and curriculum isn't the only aspect of education that causes attrition. It's also the way students are treated in school. A National Economic and Social Rights Initiative study of "school safety" practices in New York City found that "Because students of color are concentrated in schools with fewer resources, they receive fewer supportive interventions, such as mediation or counseling, leaving teachers with fewer options for alternatives to suspension."[9]

Despite the fact that research shows that punitive measures do not improve student behavior, "Schools with the highest percentage of African American and Latino students are also more likely to be over-crowded, to have metal detectors and police personnel, and to have higher suspension rates than less crowded schools."[10]

In case there is any ambiguity about the racial implications of what is going on with policing in the schools, the report summarizes it clearly: "It is important to highlight that African American students are sus-pended more often and receive more severe punishments than White students for the same infractions."[11]

Is it any wonder that young people—particularly black young peo-ple—do not want to attend institutions like these? Instead of being celebrated and supported, they are being policed and punished.

Tragically, for young people who don't graduate, the numbers sent to prison are far higher. Incarceration rates are nearly *fifty times the na-tional average* for African Americans in their twenties and thirties who have dropped out of high school.[12] While not as stark, the incarceration rate is almost ten times higher than the national average for Latino and white men who have not graduated from high school.[13]

In the shadows of these daunting statistics, many young people strive to do their best despite the systemic barriers. Some encounter caring adults who, either informally or professionally, try to increase their chances of success. Yet too often, both the young people and the adults attempting to help them are unable to overcome the societal obstacles.

Many adults in positions of power in schools and other youth-service settings view the young people they work with in negative, deficit-oriented ways. For instance, the Texas Youth Commission has developed a "resocialization" program "to address biological factors and underly-ing emotional dynamics that fuel delinquent behaviors [and] to remove cognitive justifications used by youth for continued delinquency."[14] The program requires young people to admit and abandon "thinking errors" such as "feeling special."[15]

Staff from the Texas Youth Commission have been invited to train other states' employees in implementing the "resocialization" program.

Across the country, deficit-oriented models like this exist and bureaucrats are paid to argue about how to help "these kids." Young peoples' strengths and talents rarely receive much more than lip service. Whether they are seen as criminals or victims, not much is expected from them.

Once institutions are established, they generally have a limited capacity to be responsive to young people. They are *institutions*, after all, with rules and procedures that, while not literally etched in stone, are certainly slow and complicated to change. Even when caring, intelligent people populate the staffs of schools and youth programs, too often young people end up passing through as numbers to be accommodated.

Despite positive individual relationships young people might have with adults they encounter, the institutional stance is that they are recipients of a service. Students might have the opportunity to pick which school elective they want to enroll in, but it is much less frequent that they are welcomed into decision-making processes that have a profound effect on their experience or the institution itself.

## CHANGE RULES

Not only is it hard to change the way institutions are run, but the academic curriculum within our schools is similarly calcified. The bulk of the schools in this country still operate with what Brazilian educational theorist Paulo Freire dubbed the "banking model" of education, in which students are seen as empty vessels waiting for deposits of information.

"Implicit in the banking concept is the assumption of a dichotomy between man and the world: man is merely *in* the world, not *with* the world or with others; man is spectator, not re-creator."[16] Just as students are not included in shaping the institutions they are a part of, they are also excluded from playing a role—other than, perhaps, as a receptacle—in their own learning.

The standardized curriculum and delivery methods that are pervasive in our public schools not only risk boring young people out the door, they also fail to prepare the students who remain. Philosopher and educator John Dewey explained in 1938 that traditional schooling presents an "essentially static . . . finished product, with little regard either to the ways in which it was originally built up or to the changes that will surely occur in the future."

Dewey refers to traditional schooling as "a cultural product of societies that assumed the future would be much like the past." And yet, as early as the 1930s, he was able to point out that such traditional schooling is mistakenly "used as educational food in a society where change is the rule, not the exception."[17]

Many hip-hop artists share Dewey's disdain for the "essentially static." In the mid-nineties, graffiti legend Futura 2000 explained to a friend that writing on trains and walls was no longer "hip-hop." What? Graffiti was widely known as one of the four main elements of hip-hop, and trains and walls had always been the canvases of choice. And now one of its pioneers was declaring it not to be hip-hop?

It was only hip-hop before anyone else was doing it, Futura explained. So then what had hip-hop visual art become in the nineties? Getting up on the Internet. Futura had begun exploring digital tunnels where he could paint his name and iconic characters.[18] Given that this conversation occurred over a decade ago, one can only imagine what Futura might consider hip hop art now.

The imperative for innovation is not unique to hip-hop. Four thousand years ago, the Egyptian scribe Khakheperresenb chiseled in stone: "Would I had phrases that are not known, utterances that are strange, in new language that has not been used, free from repetition, not an utterance which has grown stale."[19] The quest to be fresh is, in some sense, timeless.

But in hip-hop, the passion for originality goes beyond the "innovation-as-mandate" principle shared by other artistic and scientific movements. In suggesting guiding principles of hip-hop aesthetics in his essay "On Lit Hop," Adam Mansbach describes the "frenetic learning curve" that has driven generations of hip-hoppers: "Train pieces and rhymes and musical productions became fodder for what was to come next at the exact moment of their completion, going from innovative to passé in the blink of an eye because of the sheer intellectual force of every kid clocking and biting and scheming on how to take it one step further, chop those wild-style letter segments or that rhyme scheme or that drum loop just a little bit flyer."[20]

The premium that hip-hop places on rapid and relentless evolution makes perfect sense in a society that, as Dewey pointed out, is constantly changing. Both Dewey's concern about an educational model that fails to adapt and the relevance of hip-hop's continuous metamorphosis are ever more salient now, given the ways in which technological advances and globalization have accelerated the rate of societal change.

For the past half-century, computer engineers have kept up with Moore's law, which states that the number of transistors that can be placed on an integrated circuit doubles every two years. This explains why every time one buys a computer, camera, or MP3 player it has twice as much memory as the last time; why phones now can do more than desktop computers could do ten years ago; why today people can carry more data in their pocket than could fit in the Brooklyn Public Library a hundred years ago.

Not only is change the norm, as opposed to an exception, but *exponential change is the rule*. Where does this leave our students? If one accepts the premise that there are a finite number of jobs available, how are they going to compete for those jobs when they are not only going up against their privileged peers in this continent, but also against millions of young people all over the world, as well as computers that have automated many jobs?

Even the depressingly low percentage of students who make it through the school system are in trouble. They have a diploma in hand, but what have they been prepared for?

A 2005 survey of young people who had recently graduated from public high schools found that 39 percent of those who were employed felt unprepared for their positions. Their employers made the exact same assessment, on average estimating that 39 percent of recent graduates were "unprepared for the expectations that they face in entry-level jobs." Forty-nine percent of the above graduates' unemployed peers reported that they had gaps in the skills and abilities they would need for the jobs they hoped to obtain.[21]

Attending and graduating from college may help these young people acquire jobs, but are they leaving high school prepared for the college experience? The same report cited above, which was commissioned by Achieve, Inc., asked a cohort of college students to evaluate their own level of preparation for college based on six factors. "Only 14% of college students feel that they are generally able to do what is expected of them in all six dimensions," the report found. Fifty-six percent of these students reported that "high school left them unprepared for the work and study habits expected in college."[22]

At the end of the Achieve report, a set of measures is suggested to better prepare students for college and employment. Ninety-seven percent of the college students surveyed felt they would be better prepared if they had more "opportunities for real-world learning and making coursework more relevant." Ninety-five percent of the employers surveyed agreed.[23]

Schools that utilize project-based learning are in a good position to offer students such opportunities. Although there are scenarios in which teachers assign projects that are contrived and irrelevant, the style of project-based learning employed by schools such as HSRA facilitates student work that is grounded in timely interests and real-world experiences.

For instance in chapter 1, the students involved in Click4Life interacted with elected officials and businesspeople on work that changed state laws and affected peoples' lives, and the students in the Sweat Equity Enterprises Design partnership interacted with professional designers to develop products that could be taken to market. In chapter 2, Lil C collaborated with a lawyer to develop a release form so that she could publish the book she was writing without facing legal consequences, and she created a song to submit for the soundtrack of a major motion picture.

The other remedies proposed at the end of the Achieve report centered on increasing standardized testing, as well as the quantity and difficulty of course work.[24] Mainstream education reform organizations, foundations, and the federal Department of Education have chosen to focus the bulk of their resources on some of the very same solutions: ratcheting up the magnitude and rigor of traditional classroom-based study, and raising the number and stakes of tests administered—these are the deposits and withdrawals of the banking model of education described by Freire.

In environments focused on course work in core academic subject areas and test results that drastically affect the futures of students, staff, and the school itself, it is difficult for schools that favor student-led learning to exist. Survival becomes even harder for such schools during financial recessions. While economic shortfalls lead to challenges for all schools, those furthest from the mainstream are often hit first and hardest.

## WHEN THE CASH FLOW SLOWS

The 2009–10 school year started with bad news for Minnesota educators. The state was looking at a multibillion-dollar deficit and the governor, Tim Pawlenty, who prides himself on being a "fiscal conservative," was determined not to raise taxes. But the state is required by law to close out every year with a balanced budget, so something had to be done with the biggest line items.

Pawlenty did not have the political capital or will to openly slash spending on education. Rather than drastically cut the state's education budget, the governor decided to hold back 27.5 percent of schools' funds until the first half of the following school year—a solution only insofar as it delayed the problem. This drove many schools to immediately take out loans in order to cover basic costs such as teachers' salaries. In turn, the schools had to use taxpayers' dollars that were intended for students to instead pay interest on these loans.

Charters and other small schools were affected particularly harshly because they run on lean budgets with few areas of spending that can be deferred. HSRA, which in its previous twelve years never had to borrow money, was forced to take out a line of credit. The school also had to budget conservatively and students and staff worked hard to raise additional funds, which helped close the funding gap left by the state.

Unfortunately, foundations, corporations, and other potential funders are reluctant to offer significant support to schools when those schools' main funding streams look unreliable. A corporate sponsor was considering a $5 million investment in a new facility for HSRA, but they got cold feet upon discovering that the state would be expanding the budget holdback to 30 percent for the 2010–11 school year. They have seen that as banks tighten lending, some schools cannot secure the level of borrowing necessary to stay afloat, and they do not want to make a large gift to a school that may not be able to keep its doors open.

The financial challenges resulting from the state's budget shortfall and the governor's decisions threaten to disrupt the very DNA of HSRA's program. With fewer dollars, advisory sizes grow, hours shorten, books cannot be purchased, and trips are cancelled.

## NAME CALLING

When Barack Obama was campaigning for president he promised that, if elected, his administration would hold administrators, teachers, parents, and students accountable. He also promised that he would reform George W. Bush's 2001 No Child Left Behind Act, so that the government would support schools in need of improvement, rather than punishing them.

The American Recovery and Reinvestment Act (commonly known as "the stimulus plan"), signed into law in the beginning of 2009, included $90.9 billion for education, $5 billion of which came in the form of discretionary funds that the federal Department of Education chose to distribute to states on a competitive basis. Some of those funds are currently being allotted through School Improvement Grants.

Part of how the grant amounts are calculated is based on the number of "persistently low-achieving schools" in the state requesting funds. Obama was making good on his promise—schools in need of improvement would get support, an especially attractive possibility for schools in Minnesota, given the state budget issues described above.

The problem with this approach is that it rewards states for designating a larger number of schools as "low achieving." Such a designation is demoralizing to educators, students, and families. And it makes it difficult to attract community support, foundation funding, corporate partnership, and talented staff members.

In addition to the negative connotations of the terminology, being designated as "low achieving" sends schools into "corrective action." External consultants come in to assess the school and recommend improvement models. Possible recommendations include "turnaround," which entails replacing the principal and at least half the teachers; "transformation," which requires replacing the principal and reforming the curriculum; and all-out closure. Some schools may need such drastic actions. Other schools do not.

Many educators around the country have found a solution to ensure that their school will not face the consequences of being deemed "low achieving." Since the designation is made based on metrics such as test scores, attendance, and graduation rates, the quickest way to guarantee good numbers is to push out students who jeopardize the desired statistics.

A study of high-stakes accountability systems found that such methods lead "not to equitable educational possibilities for youth, but to avoidable losses of thousands of youth from our schools."[25] Principals' job security and, in some states, salary bonuses are attached to these numbers. So, rather than risk their livelihood, some find ways of getting rid of students whom they believe will not perform well.

Schools that actually try hard to keep their most troubled students or that have the gumption to go a step further and seek out young people who have been jettisoned by other schools are being penalized when the numbers are tallied. As if educating students whose lives are thick with trauma is not difficult enough, these schools end up experiencing assaults on their existence.

This is what recently happened to HSRA. In hopes of receiving federal funds through a School Improvement Grant, the Minnesota Department of Education placed HSRA on a list of "persistently low-achieving schools." The irony is that HSRA was placed on the list for doing the very thing the school proposed to do in its charter application—serve highly mobile, overaged, under-credited dropouts.

Sounds crazy, right? Here's what went down: Based on federal criteria, Minnesota designated any school that had a four-year graduation rate of lower than 60 percent as a "low-achieving school." But the way the state calculates the graduation rate is based on an inelastic four-year timeline from when a student begins high school. What about the thousands of students who drop out or are kicked out of the comprehensive high schools around the city or for other reasons fall behind in their studies?

Consider a student like Josh,[26] who enrolled at HSRA in the early months of 2010, having spent four years at Gordon Parks High School, which is an "alternative learning program" in St. Paul.[27] After some staff changes at Gordon Parks, Josh says he felt "the teachers didn't believe in me, and I didn't believe in myself." So he left the school.

Determined to be the first person in his family to graduate from high school "outside of prison or a GED," Josh took it upon himself to enroll at HSRA. Despite a busy work schedule at a home for people with physical disabilities, Josh is on track to graduate in the fall of 2010 and is planning to pursue a career in counseling.

But guess what? As far as the state is concerned, Josh contributes to the percentage of students HSRA "failed" to graduate within four years, because *before he joined the school* his four-year countdown had already run out. The formula for judging the quality of an individual school by calculating students' graduation rates from the beginning of their high school experience—even if it's somewhere else—does not account for students who have switched schools during their high school career.

This is wildly unfair to students like Josh and to the educators at HSRA who work hard to serve him and his peers. It means that there is no way, based on the numbers, to distinguish between a "dropout factory" and a *dropout recovery program.*

States such as New York and California have noted this issue and taken it into account when determining which schools they consider "low achieving." A guideline from the federal government allows and suggests that an exception be made for "schools specifically designed to serve overage, under-credited students" when identifying "low-achieving schools."

Minnesota took this advice and excluded from the list alternative learning programs that did not have high enough graduate rates. But, even though 95 percent of HSRA students meet the criteria for admission to alternative learning programs, the state was unwilling to exclude HSRA due to its status as a charter school.

This is especially ironic given that many students, like Josh, actually came to HSRA after dropping out of alternative learning programs. So despite the fact that HSRA serves students that slipped through the cracks of alternative learning programs, they were not given the same immunity from the "low-achieving" albatross.

The school community was upset by the designation. While many students at HSRA are used to being stigmatized by government agencies, the insult still stung. But the primary emotional response was fear. Students worried that the school would be closed or that the staff with whom they had formed relationships would be gone.

Would this be the end to Josh's dream of being the first person in his family to graduate? This was not a hypothetical question—it was a burning concern to Josh, his mother, and the staff at HSRA.

Besides causing alarm in the school community, the "low-achieving" designation created other problems. The media picked up on it. Rather than engaging in investigative journalism about the criteria of the "low-achieving" designation, most just printed lists of the schools with the implicit assumption that whatever methodology was used to determine schools' status was sound.

This publicity was harmful to the reputations of the schools on the list. HSRA has worked hard over the years to cultivate relationships with individual and corporate donors. One can imagine the response when an executive at LubeTech (one of HSRA's sponsors) invited a colleague to the annual HSRA fundraiser . . . "But isn't that one of the low-achieving schools?"

The school's board appealed to the state department of education to be removed from the list, but the department would not budge. So the school's leaders went to state legislators and made their case. Several of the legislators were sympathetic, but it turned out they couldn't force the Minnesota Department of Education to change anything.

"The common knowledge among schools in Minnesota is that the Department of Education is so powerful that you just can't fight them," explained Tony Simmons, HSRA's director of development. This is where school founder David "TC" Ellis's relentless hustle, confidence, and inclination for collaboration kicked in.[28]

HSRA would not roll over for the state department of education. They would fight and they would win, even if he had to do something he rarely did—put on a suit. For the next four months, Simmons and Ellis spent every day focused on this issue.

They dedicated over six hundred hours and employed multiple strategies, including frequent trips to the state capitol to engage directly with the Minnesota Department of Education; communication with and visits to the federal Department of Education; numerous conversations with state legislators, education policy experts, and lawyers; and drafting a bill amendment.

Eventually, the Minnesota Department of Education offered HSRA a waiver from the "persistently low-achieving" list. While this was undeniably a victory, it was a formidable drain of time that could have gone to supporting and improving the operations of the school.

"If it ain't one thing, it's another," TC said. "They've been trying to shut the school down since we started." From charter reviews to audits to the "adequate yearly progress" benchmarks dictated by the No Child Left Behind Act, over the years the state has threatened HSRA's existence many times. None of these threats have stopped the school from moving forward on its mission, but they have taken their toll on the community, exhausting staff time and focus, upsetting students and families, and taking the place of more meaningful measurements and assessments.

While the details of these battles may be particular, these types of skirmishes for survival are not unique to HSRA. They are indicative of the attacks that unfairly punish and distract educators who commit to a genuine *no child left behind* policy. The price that HSRA and these other schools pay for their *"by any means necessary"* approach to engaging disenfranchised students makes one thing clear: When you're on the cutting edge, sometimes you bleed.

## NOTES

1. Christopher B. Swanson and Amy M. Hightower, "Diplomas Count 2008," PowerPoint Slide 4, http://www.edweek.org/media/ew/dc/2008/DC08_Presentation_FINAL.pdf (accessed December 16, 2010).

2. Swanson and Hightower, "Diplomas Count 2008," PowerPoint Slide 11.

3. Swanson and Hightower, "Diplomas Count 2008," PowerPoint Slide 11.

4. Christopher B. Swanson, "Who Graduates, Who Doesn't? A Statistical Portrait of Public High School Graduation, Class of 2001," *Urban Institute Education Policy Center*, 32, http://www.urban.org/UploadedPDF/410934_WhoGraduates.pdf (accessed December 17, 2010).

5. Swanson, "Who Graduates, Who Doesn't?" vi.

6. American Psychological Association, "Facing the school dropout dilemma" (2010): 5, http://www.apa.org/pi/families/resources/school-dropout-prevention.pdf (accessed December 17, 2010).

7. Swanson, "Who Graduates, Who Doesn't?" 28.

8. Ethan Yazzie-Mintz, "Voices of Students on Engagement: A Report on the 2006 High School Survey of Student Engagement," Center for Evaluation

and Education Policy Indiana University (2006): 5, http://www.eric.ed.gov:80/
PDFS/ED495758.pdf (accessed January 13, 2011).

9. Elizabeth Sullivan and Elizabeth Keeney, "Teachers Talk: School Culture, Safety and Human Rights," National Economic and Social Rights Initiative and Teachers Unite, (2008): 3, http://www.nesri.org/Teachers_Talk.pdf
(accessed December 17, 2010).

10. Sullivan and Keeney, "Teachers Talk."

11. Sullivan and Keeney, "Teachers Talk"

12. Bruce Western, *Punishment and Inequality in America* (New York: Russell Sage Foundation, 2006): 18.

13. Western, *Punishment and Inequality in America*, 17.

14. Texas Youth Commission, "Resocialization: The Rehabilitation Model"
http://www.tyc.state.tx.us/programs/resocial.html (accessed December 17,
2010).

15. Texas Youth Commission "Family Guide to Resocialization" http://www
.tyc.state.tx.us/archive/programs/familyguide/family7.html (accessed December 17, 2010).

16. Paulo Freire, *Pedagogy of the Oppressed* (New York: Herder and
Herder, 1971), 62.

17. John Dewey, *Experience & Education*, (New York: Collier Books, 1963),
19.

18. Sam Spitzer, in discussion with the author, 2001.

19. James Gleick, *Genius: The Life and Science of Richard Feynman* (New
York: Pantheon Books, 1992), 326, attributed to Khakheperresenb, quoted in
Lentricchia (1980), 318.

20. Adam Mansbach, "On Lit Hop," in *Total Chaos: The Art and Aesthetics
of Hip-Hop*, ed. Jeff Chang (New York: Basic Civitas, 2006), 93–94.

21. Peter D. Hart Research Associates/Public Opinion Strategies, "Rising to
the Challenge: Are High School Graduates Prepared for College and Work?"
Achieve, Inc. (2005): 3, http://www.achieve.org/files/pollreport_0.pdf (accessed
January 13, 2011).

22. "Rising to the Challenge," 4.

23. "Rising to the Challenge," 13.

24. "Rising to the Challenge."

25. Linda M. McNeil, Eileen Coppola, Judy Radigan, and Julian V. Hei-
lig, "Avoidable Losses: High-Stakes Accountability and the Dropout Crisis,"
*Education Policy Analysis Archives 16(3)*, (2008): 2, http://epaa.asu.edu/epaa/
v16n3/ (accessed December 17, 2010).

26. Josh's last name is omitted to protect his anonymity.

27. Alternative learning programs, commonly referred to as area learning centers in St. Paul, offer alternative teaching methods and flexible hours in nontraditional learning environments.

28. For a more complete description of TC Ellis's leadership qualities, see chapter 3.

# (5)

# TRENDS IN HIP-HOP EDUCATION

Do we realize how much power hip-hop has? The hip-hop generation can take a stand collectively and make a statement. There are
a lot of people who are doing something positive, who are doing
hip-hop the way it was meant to be done. They are reaching young
people showing them what the world could be.

—Kool Herc

For the graffiti artists, tagging walls wasn't about mimicking art
school technique or being self-consciously postmodern. For the His-
panic breakers, it wasn't about simply departing from the traditions
of Latin social dancing with its rigorous turns and upright posture.
For DJs, break spinning wasn't some departure from the norms of
soul music. For all these old-schoolers it was an accidental, offhand
discovery of a way to distinguish themselves in a very direct, self-
contained, and totally controllable way. They needed simple tools to
make their art and they made their own decisions about what made
it good.

—Nelson George

**S**ituating the High School for Recording Arts (HSRA) in multiple contexts gives the clearest picture of the school and the best perspective

from which to consider the implications of Hip Hop Genius. Whereas chapter 4 provided a societal context by discussing some of the systemic challenges faced by HSRA's students and the institution itself, this chapter focuses on the growing field of hip-hop education. By profiling some of the trends in the field, this chapter locates HSRA's particular blend of hip-hop music, culture, and ingenuity.

Like any other field, hip-hop education contains a variety of value systems that manifest in a diverse set of techniques. All of the methods profiled in this chapter were developed with the intention of engaging and educating students, but some may be perceived as reductive or corny in their understanding of hip-hop, while others may come across as if they emerge from a deep understanding of hip-hop's intricacies. In order to place HSRA's work and the concept of Hip Hop Genius in the vast field of education, it is necessary to consider all of these approaches.

Many experts on hip-hop education are not mentioned below—most importantly students and teachers who are engaged in hip-hop teaching and learning on a regular basis, but do not spend time writing about and publicizing their work. As happens in most arenas, a disproportionate percentage of the props end up going to academics who study and write about aspects of the work. Some innovators are lauded, while others whose contributions are just as valuable, if not more so, go unrecognized. These are the pioneers who stayed up late transcribing rap lyrics before the Internet provided tomes of such poems, who walked school hallways with karaoke machines bungee-corded to laundry carts, who slid desks to the sides of classrooms to create dance floors, and who turned cement walls of afterschool centers into vertical visual playgrounds. It is because of and in honor of these groundbreakers that hip-hop education must be both defended and defined.

## FROM DEFENDING TO DEFINING HIP-HOP EDUCATION

A chart hangs on a classroom door at the state juvenile detention center in Cranston, Rhode Island. Its crooked stenciled letters inform students how many "points" they will lose for engaging in various activities. "Talking back" to the teacher costs three points; using curse words costs a student four points; *rapping costs five.* That poster-sized piece of card-stock illustrates a message: It is not that other educators don't recognize how powerful hip-hop can be—it is that they understand its potential and are scared of it.

Why are administrators and teachers afraid? Some view hip-hop as a negative influence in students' lives. As far as they are concerned, hip-hop music promotes violence, misogyny, homophobia, hypercapitalist consumption, and—to add insult to injury for the English teachers—bad grammar.

Hip-hop culture is seen as a force that competes for students' attention, which frustrates some teachers who invest time and energy attempting to engage students, only to be drowned out by cultural products that often critique the very values their schools are trying to instill.

Layers of racism, classism, and ageism also fuel some educators' negative responses to a cultural form created predominantly by black and Latino young people from low-income communities. This is likely magnified by how incredibly successful hip-hop is at engaging the very students that these same educators are unable—or, in some cases, unwilling—to reach.

In such hostile climates, it took courage for the first hip-hop educators to enter schools with boomboxes, linoleum mats, and graffiti magazines. It took tireless optimism for youth program administrators to write grants to start DJing and urban fashion design workshops.

Instructors had to justify every song they wanted to play, every guest they invited, every rhyme they allowed students to write, the way they embraced and spoke with students, the tilt of their hat and sag of their pants. They brought hip-hop culture into the classroom *despite* the systems and institutions they worked in—the potential for saving lives was too real.

For this reason and others, there has been explosive growth in the field of hip-hop education over the last several years. Hundreds of people have begun incorporating hip-hop music, culture, and sensibilities into their work as educators and education into their work as hip-hoppers. Some came up through academia, got certified as teachers, and then discovered hip-hop and the power it held in their work with young people; others were longtime hip-hop heads, who knew when they entered the profession that engaging hip-hop would be a central part of their work with students; while others found their way into classrooms through their reputations and relationships in the hip-hop community.

Regardless of how they came to it, these educators now find themselves defending the role of hip-hop music and culture. While the proliferation of hip-hop education may have chipped away at the notion that hip-hop is dangerous, there is still a battle being fought over whether it has educational merit. Cultural critic Bakari Kitwana observes: "I see hip-hop generationers who are parents, educators, artists and activists excited about the possibilities for hip-hop being used as a tool to reach students in elementary and high schools. Elite educators are concerned about the testing of such curriculum to measure its effectiveness, but hip-hop artists/educators are convinced if it helps students to connect to the material and get excited about learning, that's half the battle."[1]

A growing body of literature makes the case that hip-hop has an important, even essential, place in education. Scholars and practitioners appeal to readers from outside the hip-hop culture to "Get Hip to Hip-Hop," while hustling to assemble arguments and evidence that hip-hop is a valid literary form, a culture worthy of academic attention, and an effective instructional tool.[2]

In his essay "The Culture of Hip-Hop," sociology professor and prolific author on race and culture Michael Eric Dyson argues that rap music is rich with literary traditions and historical information.

"Rap expresses the ongoing preoccupation with literacy and orality that has characterized African-American communities since the inception of legally coerced illiteracy during slavery," Dyson explains. "Rap artists explore grammatical creativity, verbal wizardry, and linguistic innovation in refining the art of oral communication."

Dyson writes about how "rap has retrieved historic black ideas, movements, and figures" and posits that "this renewed historicism permits young blacks to discern links between the past and their own present circumstances, using the past as a fertile source of social reflection, cultural creation, and political resistance."[3]

"Regarding twenty-first century urban public school classroom instruction, what is more culturally responsive than Hip Hop?" asks education doctoral student Keisha Green in the Hip-Hop Association's *Hip-Hop Education Guidebook*. Green goes on to relate personal experiences as a high school English instructor in New York City, in an effort to demonstrate how "culturally responsive teaching and learning practices significantly enhance student academic achievement and overall engagement, particularly among black and brown students."[4]

Green explains how, in her class, hip-hop served as a "bridge between [students'] lived experiences, prior knowledge, and academic literacy." By designing a curriculum that related and compared the writings of Langston Hughes and Lorraine Hansberry to contemporary rap lyrics, Green "hooked" her students, "who, as a result willingly participated in classroom discussions and responded to the readings through essays that were written passionately and skillfully."[5]

As Green's example illustrates, much of hip-hop education thus far has been thought about within the context of classrooms in relatively conventional schools and out-of-school programs. Even more specifically, most often, hip-hop education has meant the study, analysis, and creation of texts—generally rap lyrics, videos, or films. This prioritization of the textual components of hip-hop over the visual or physical elements—reflect society's privileging of cultural products that are easily monetized, such as CDs, DVDs, and MP3s, as well as schools' obsession with literary skills over all other forms of intelligence.

As the field has grown, practitioners and scholars have begun to document a variety of creative approaches to integrating hip-hop and education. Out of this wide range of methods, some overlapping trends have emerged, including using hip-hop as bait to get students in through the door of the classroom, studying hip-hop art as content, looking to hip-hop as fertile grounds for social justice education, and engaging hip-hop texts to investigate issues of identity with students.

## USING HIP-HOP:
## THE PEANUT BUTTER AND THE PILL

Dogs hate pills. So, when a dog falls ill, how do you get it to take its medicine? One trick is to dip a spoon into a jar of peanut butter and then bury the pill in the lump of sweet saltiness. The dog will then lick at the spoon until all the peanut butter, and the pill, is swallowed.

The motivation of many educators who have turned to hip-hop is not to delve into the intrinsic values and lessons that the culture holds.

Instead, teachers attempt to use hip-hop music and culture as peanut butter to get students to swallow pills—playing a rap song at the beginning of a class about poetry, while only making cursory efforts to find—or better yet, to ask students to find—connections between the song and the lesson.

There is no doubt that an opportunity to engage with hip-hop art can be a motivating factor for many students. HSRA has found that granting "All Access" passes to the school's recording studios on a weekly basis contingent upon each student's attendance and completion of tasks on their learning plan improves students' performance. But this is only one strand of the complex web of ways in which HSRA builds around hip-hop culture. There are inherent risks when schools use hip-hop as peanut butter and nothing more.

Just check out the language here: *Using* hip-hop. This is often the first instinct educators have when they begin to consider hip-hop's efficacy. A teacher uses Tupac (or fill in the rapper of choice) to try to lure students into studying Shakespeare (or fill in the traditionally valued writer of choice). It is not that such activities cannot be effective; it is that there are a number of unsafe assumptions that go into such a move.

One assumption is that students will relate to Tupac's music. Just because a student is a sixteen-year-old black male who lives in an urban community doesn't mean he listens to rap music. And, just because a student listens to rap music, does not mean she likes *all* rap music. Students of different ages from different areas of the country listen to different artists. For some students, 'Pac is not going to be peanut butter.

The final, potentially most harmful assumption is that students are like dogs that adults have the right to trick into swallowing something. There are times when students may resist doing certain things that are good for them, but the solution must be much more dynamic and authentic than bribing them using the Tupac–Shakespeare bump and switch.

## HIP-HOP AS CONNECTION, CONTENT, AND CONDUIT

Some educators have combined the immediate interest hip-hop music can evoke with comparative and critical analysis of literary arts. California's 2007 Teacher of the Year Alan Lawrence Sitomer and the executive director of Urban Word NYC Michael Cirelli published *Hip-Hop Poetry and the Classics*, a book that provides teachers with lesson plans and worksheets that build on hip-hop's appeal to interest young people in "classic poetry," and on classic poetry's esteem to validate hip-hop's literary merits.[6]

The standards-aligned curriculum is intended to excite students about the complex meaning, power, and beauty of the written and spoken word while also aiming to teach them literary devices and analytical skills. These skills prepare students for success on standardized tests and, more importantly, they enrich students' experiences engaging with cultural products and media, as students develop new methods of interpretation and analysis.

Although these sorts of curricula can be extremely useful for English teachers overwhelmed by trying to build engaging lessons into state standards, there can be a problematic value judgment built in — generally by the authors of the standards and not the hip-hop educators — that what all students really need to read is "the classics." This is a manifestation of the commonly held belief in a canon of content —written almost entirely by white men who are no longer living—that all students need to know. The enforcement of such beliefs can alienate students, deny educators the freedom to be creative, prevent students from being exposed to many excellent texts, and perpetuate racism, classism, sexism, and other systems of hateration.

In *Hip-Hop Poetry and the Classics*, Sitomer and Cirelli challenge this sort of hegemony, overtly calling existing power structures into question by inviting students to analyze lyrics from songs such as Public Enemy's "Fight the Power" and Tupac's "Me against the World." As their book demonstrates, hip-hop can be more than bait.

Rapper Gabriel "Asheru" Benn and his colleague Rick Henning have developed a catalog of "culturally relevant teaching materials" based on rap lyrics.[7] Their company, Educational Lyrics, creates National Reading Standards–aligned student workbooks, teachers' guides, and assessments that aim to improve student literacy without tying into canonical texts.[8] Each workbook focuses on one rap song, such as "The Ghetto" by Rakim or "Bridging the Gap" by Nas and his father Olu Dara, and provides more than sixty reading and writing activities stemming from the text.

Rather than referring to songs and lyrics by established rap artists, some teachers and students have organically developed raps, dances, and multimedia productions to communicate concepts that students are expected to learn and remember. In search of hip-hop materials that engage students, provide rich learning opportunities, and carry standards-aligned information and ideas, others have turned to a growing industry of nonprofits and companies who create CDs and complementary workbooks, offering them online with downloadable purchase orders for school administrators' convenience.

The website Mathraps.com advertises CDs by the Rappin' Mathematician, who on one volume kicks rhymes about a wide range of topics, including "Geometric Shapes, Math Vocabulary, Saying NO to Drugs, . . . Parts of a Circle [and] Not Believing Everything on TV."[9] Other companies, such as Rhythm Rhyme Results and Flocabulary offer an array of textbooks and accompanying CDs on language arts, social studies, math, and science.[10]

Unlike the Rappin' Mathematician and Flocabulary, Smart Shorties, a subsidiary of the Scholastic publishing company, engages students in the *production* of songs and videos that teach mathematical concepts.[11] With the guidance of an experienced teacher and a pop music producer, a small group of students craft catchy lyrics and set them to the most popular rap beats of the moment. These songs are then sold to schools, where students are encouraged to memorize their peers' creations through repetition of the lyrics and choreographing dances to the songs.

A pilot study conducted by the company found that 67 percent of Smart Shorties' participants in Washington, D.C., improved their test scores.[12] The point here is not that test scores are an accurate measurement of a program's efficacy, but rather that these approaches are being marketed and measured as tools for success within established educational systems.

Similar to the Smart Shorties model, HSRA students compose original beats and lyrics to build their own mathematical knowledge while creating songs to help others learn as well. Mike Conway, one of HSRA's math facilitators, partners with Phil Winden, the school's studio director to engage students in learning math and music production skills in tandem.

As students compose beats in software programs such as ProTools and Logic, they see visual representations of sound waves. By drawing connections between the sound waves and trigonometric concepts, Mike equips students to read the visual information on their screens. This provides young producers with another source of information when making beats.

One group of students produced a half-hour radio show on the "Music of Math" that aired on the Twin Cities' commercial hip-hop station, KTTB-FM, 96.3.[13] They employed mathematical concepts, such as amplitude, frequency, and phase shift, to construct beats for songs about those very concepts.

Between playing original songs like "A Story of SOHCAHTOA" and "Speaking Statistically," students talked about the connections between math and music; and one student, "Ruby P.," demonstrated the concepts of amplitude, frequency, and phase shift through an improvisational beat-boxing routine.

Other groups of HSRA students have produced songs to teach younger learners math rules, replacing mnemonics like "Please Excuse My Dear Aunt Sally" with hip new ways to remember the order of operations. The tutoring company, Rocket Learning, has commissioned HSRA students to develop such songs. Students and staff are now considering starting their own business producing educational music.

While some of the songs that HSRA students record integrate academic subjects, HSRA provides ample opportunities for students to teach and learn the art of hip-hop lyricism and music production as an end in itself. Like their counterparts at HSRA, other educators across the country also teach hip-hop skills for the sake of deepening students' understanding, appreciation, and mastery of the art forms. This most commonly happens in the context of out-of-school programs or school electives.

Rather than inviting kids to record songs for the purpose of helping them learn math or any other traditional school subject, these educators have put together lessons that teach students how to write rhymes, freestyle, DJ, make beats, breakdance, draw and paint graffiti pieces, design apparel, and build other skills related to hip-hop culture. In these instances, the creation of hip-hop art is itself *the* subject of study.

## THE THIRD HALF

Even when teachers have the freedom to move outside the realm of standards and classics to introduce hip-hop texts and techniques on their own merits, the focus is often more on *what* is being learned than *how* learning is happening. Lesson plans that teach hip-hop skills can be highly appealing to students, as can lessons that involve analyzing popular texts, but—unless approached creatively—both kinds of lessons are more innovative in content than pedagogy.

Asking a whole class to watch a video that they find exciting and then break into groups to discuss the subject matter can be a cool, engaging, and even transformative thing for a teacher to do. But it is a classroom exercise. It is not necessarily flipping dominant educational practices.

If Kitwana is correct that getting students connected to school and excited about learning is "half the battle," the other half, which is equally important, is what to do once they're connected. A central piece of this second half is the development of literacy and numeracy skills, as described above as well as in examples from HSRA that appear in previous chapters, such as Reidun's paper defending Harry Potter and Lil C's book on astrology. Ensuring that young people develop proficiency with words and numbers is key to ensuring that they are able to live fulfilling lives.

But *how* will they acquire those skills and what other abilities and sensibilities might they develop? Once they are drawn in, will hip-hop music and culture be engaged through teaching methods that mimic the "essentially static" styles criticized by John Dewey? Or does hip-hop hold new pedagogical possibilities?

Some educators and scholars are working with students to identify approaches to teaching and learning that are unique to hip-hop. In these ways and more, hip-hop's potential to reshape educational practices may be an equally important *third half* of Kitwana's equation.

## HIP-HOP EDUCATION AS SOCIAL JUSTICE EDUCATION

The Hip-Hop Association's *Hip-Hop Education Guidebook* is arguably the most comprehensive hip-hop education text available.[14] In addition to providing lesson plans and worksheets that would fit into the trends explored above, the guidebook provides a theoretical framework for what hip-hop education should entail.

One of the authors and creators of the guidebook, Marcella Runell Hall, explores hip-hop's place in social justice education, arguing that "All hip-hop education should be grounded and contextualized in the belief that our society is characterized by oppression, which includes but is not limited to racism, classism and sexism."[15] In this context, Paulo Freire, Gloria Ladson-Billings, and Sonia Nieto are invoked, and the case is made for a shift toward social justice education, which Runell Hall describes as an "interdisciplinary, comprehensive" extension of critical pedagogy.[16]

In his essay "We Can Relate: Hip-Hop Culture, Critical Pedagogy, and the Secondary Classroom," education professor David Stovall describes several social studies lessons he facilitated in which the critical analysis of rap lyrics sparked group discussions about topics relevant to students' lives.[17] For instance, Stovall recounts linking Talib Kweli's rap remake of the song "Four Women" by Nina Simone to Howard Zinn's *Peoples' History of the United States* to initiate a conversation about historical accuracy. The class looked at the portrayals of slavery in the texts and discussed how they differed from the historical narratives generally disseminated in schools. They were asked to consider how schools promoted deception and "What would be included in a curriculum that challenged dishonesty?"[18]

A media education nonprofit, Just Think, has created a curriculum called "Flipping the Script" that answers this question by providing educators with tools to provoke students to think critically about the messages propagated by hip-hop artists and companies that associate themselves with hip-hop culture. Lesson plans delve into topics such as the ways companies covertly advertise products through hip-hop songs and the ways that hip-hop magazines and videos affect young peoples' views on sexuality and body image.

Many of Just Think's lesson plans not only have students analyze existing hip-hop texts but also ask them to create their own songs or videos. In this way, curriculums such as Flipping the Script invite students to critique systems of oppression and then develop their own alternative cultural products that subvert these systems.

Over the course of their tenure at HSRA, many students engage in a similar process of critical analysis and cultural production through "Urban Music" workshops facilitated by Darryl Young, a special education facilitator, and Phil Winden, the school's studio director. Urban Music teaches participants how to use audio production skills to make an impact on issues that affect their lives and communities.

Past Urban Music groups have produced compilation albums on topics ranging from homelessness to HIV awareness. These professional quality, mass-produced albums are distributed to audience members of all ages with targeted recipient groups depending upon the issue addressed.

The songs on each compilation represent research the students have conducted and offer multiple viewpoints on the topic, as well as their personal experiences and perspectives. These songs serve as words of inspiration and sometimes warning for their peers while also giving outsiders a glimpse at some of the challenges they face.

Urban Music carries on the hip-hop tradition of critically addressing social injustices. Although hip-hop has always included party music, it has also always told stories of experiences that were not being represented in mainstream media. Urban Music continues this legacy, teaching students how to make their songs sound good but also instilling a level of consciousness and responsibility around the message of their music.

If hip-hop education is not limited to using hip-hop culture to entice students or engaging hip-hop music as content to study for the purpose of teaching academic skills, but instead is a continuation of the traditions of popular education and critical pedagogy, then it can be a movement toward liberation. This offers students the chance to become architects of a more just destiny for themselves and their world—and it is fundamentally empowering.

As Freire states, "In order for the oppressed to be able to wage the struggle for their liberation, they must perceive the reality of oppression not as a closed world, from which there is no exit, but as a limiting situation which they can transform."[19] The work Runell-Hall, Stovall, Flipping the Script, HSRA, and others are doing to make this happen using hip-hop texts and culture is crucial to breaking systems of violence and oppression.

## IDENTITY EXPLORATION

Critically examining hip-hop texts and other media holds the promise of preparing students to be conscious consumers and creators of cultural products. But education professor Greg Dimitriadis encourages educators to let go of the "notions of control and competence that often gird . . . discussions about media literacy."[20]

Dimitriadis outlines two common problematic assumptions among media literacy educators: the first being that educators "need to teach young people to protect themselves from the pernicious effects of media," and the second being that there should be a predetermined "end point of school knowledge in mind."[21] By making these assumptions, Dimitriadis argues, educators miss important opportunities to understand young peoples' lives in more nuanced ways and overlook valuable information that could help them reconsider their own roles as teachers and thinkers.

Dimitriadis spent four years conducting one-on-one interviews and focus groups with an "almost wholly black and poor population" of young people at a community center in a small midwestern city to develop an understanding of how they interpreted and experienced hip-hop texts (which included songs, videos, and films) in their lives.[22] In his book *Performing Identity/Performing Culture: Hip-Hop as Text, Pedagogy and Lived Practice*, Dimitriadis offers an ethnographic treatment of these conversations and explores the dynamic manner in which hip-hop texts interplay with each other and with young peoples' experiences to carry out an important function in formulating knowledge and identity.

Dimitriadis points out that much media literacy work—both in and outside the hip-hop genre—treats individual texts in isolation. It does not take full account of the ways in which young people actually experience and interpret texts: in conjunction with many other texts, in relation to other people, and as influenced by their environment.

Building on Dimitriadis' foundation, education professor Marc Lamont Hill's book, *Beats, Rhymes, and Classroom Life: Hip-Hop Pedagogy and the Politics of Identity*, explores engagements of hip-hop texts in a classroom setting. Hill's book offers a participant-researcher's anthropological perspective of teaching a yearlong course called Hip-Hop Lit at an evening program for students "who do not fit comfortably within the day school environment."[23]

Hill is not only concerned with the impact that introducing hip-hop texts can have on students' academic engagement and literacy but also on the effects that studying such texts—and, in particular, studying them in a formal schooling context—can have on their identity. In turn, Hill also looks at the ways in which students' presentations and trans-formations of their identities affect relationships within the classroom.

Although the stated goals of Hill's Hip-Hop Lit course revolved around literary interpretation, analysis, and criticism, Hill structured much of the class around students' personal stories. By asking them to journal about how the song lyrics they studied related to their lives and inviting them to share their responses with the group, Hill engaged the class in a process he describes as "wounded healing," whereby students "shared their stories in ways that provided a form of release and relief for themselves and others."[24]

Eliciting such personal disclosure was intended not only to be thera-peutic but also to offer students a way to critically engage with specific texts as well as dominant narratives. Hill argues that "these practices not only defy *a priori* analyses, but also radically challenge sanctioned formations of knowledge and produce new categories of meaning."[25]

Many English and social studies teachers invite students to explore their identities through journaling and sharing stories with each other. The lyrics selected by Hill and his students provided them with entry points, content, and frames of analysis. As students developed dexterity relating to the texts, they practiced critical thinking, literary analysis, and the exploration and articulation of self-awareness.

At HSRA, self-awareness is explored, sanctioned forms of knowledge are challenged, and new categories of meaning are produced through students' creation of their own music and texts. Some students at the school choose to explicitly analyze other artists' compositions, some organically refer to previous works in their own creations, and some staff members bring song lyrics into workshops to be discussed, but the main way in which students experience release and relief, and present and explore their identities, is through assuming the role of artist and author.

There is an empowering and generative quality to such practices, as they avoid the preordained, teacher-determined end point about which Dimitriadis cautions. But there are also risks that come with encouraging such personal engagement with and creation of texts. Hill relays a story in which he introduces song lyrics about abortion and pushes a female student to share her analysis. Eventually, he realizes that she does not want to discuss the text because of her personal experience with abortion, but by the time he figures this out, she is upset and ends up disappearing from school for seven days.

"By linking the curriculum to the lived realities of the students, particularly those from marginalized groups, we position ourselves to hear stories of pain . . . that are often difficult to hear and even more difficult to tell," Hill warns.[26]

While the disconnect that students commonly feel between their identities and their academic experiences is in many ways a barrier to engagement and academic success, there is a new set of risks and responsibilities once students feel their identities are bound up in their schoolwork. This is true whether students are analyzing and reflecting on texts by others or creating their own works of art.

In the final section of his book, Hill discusses possible meanings of "hip-hop pedagogies": "In addition to using hip-hop as a scaffold for teaching traditional skills, educators must also draw from the alternative forms of knowledge and new categories of meaning that are produced through a pedagogical engagement with hip-hop culture. . . . [For instance,] How could the notion of a 'hip-hop cipher,' which marks the democratic ethos of hip-hop culture, allow us to reimagine classroom participation?"[27]

These are the sorts of questions that must now be contemplated. Hill limits his query to locating "new sites of educational possibility within hip-hop based-classrooms," but it is time to go further.[28] It is time to call into question not only what happens within classrooms but also whether classrooms are needed at all.

This is the Hip Hop Genius approach to education. No structure or convention should be viewed as unchangeable. As HSRA demonstrates, entire institutions can be reimagined and reconfigured. From promising new possibilities to explore within the context of classrooms to a fresh examination of the overall structure of schooling, the time has come to approach the field of hip-hop education in a more holistic light.

## NOTES

1. Bakari Kitwana, as quoted in Paul Farber, "Hip Hop High," originally in *Philadelphia Weekly*, www.iahhe.org/HipHopHigh.pdf (accessed December 17, 2010).

2. Edward DeJesus, *Makin' It: The Hip-Hop Guide to True Survival* (Gaithersburg, Md.: Youth Development and Research Fund, 2003), 7.

3. Michael Eric Dyson, *The Michael Eric Dyson Reader* (New York: Basic Civitas, 2004), 408–10.

4. Keisha Green, "Check It: Reflections on Hip-Hop & Education," in *The Hip-Hop Education Guidebook*, Vol. 1, ed. Tatiana Forero Puerta, Marcella Runell, and Martha Diaz (New York: Hip-Hop Association, 2007), 20.

5. Green, "Check It," 21.

6. Michael Cirelli and Alan Lawrence Sitomer, *Hip-Hop Poetry and the Classics for the Classroom* (Beverly Hills, Calif.: Milk Mug, 2004).

7. Educational Lyrics, "About Educational Lyrics," http://edlyrics.com/about-h-e-1-p/about-educational-lyrics/ (accessed December 17, 2010).

8. Educational Lyrics, "What is H.E.L.P.?" http://edlyrics.com/about-h-e-l-p/what-is-h-e-l-p/ (accessed January 13, 2011).

9. The Rappin' Mathematician, "The Rappin' Mathematician Volume 1," http://mathraps.com/volume_1.htm (accessed February 18, 2009).

10. Rhythm Rhyme Results, http://www.educationalrap.com/ (accessed December 17, 2010); and Flocabulary, http://www.flocabulary.com (accessed December 17, 2010).

11. Smart Shorties, www.smartshorties.com (accessed December 17, 2010).

12. Scholastic, "Musical Math," http://www2.scholastic.com/browse/article.jsp?id=3750328 (accessed December 17, 2010).

13. To hear the "Music of Math" radio program, which aired on KTTB-FM, 96.3, Minneapolis/St. Paul on June 8, 2008, visit http://www.thefoshow.com/2008/06/09/the-fo-show-episode-37-math-of-music/ (accessed December 17, 2010).

14. Puerta, Runell, and Diaz, *The Hip-Hop Education Guidebook*.

15. Marcella Runell, "The Organic Connection between Hip-Hop and Social Justice Education," in *The Hip-Hop Education Guidebook*, 60.

16. Marcella Runell Hall, in discussion with the author, October 2009.

17. David Stovall, "We Can Relate: Hip-Hop Culture, Critical Pedagogy, and the Secondary Classroom," *Urban Education* 41, no. 6 (2006): 585.

18. Stovall, "We Can Relate," 596–97.

19. Paulo Freire, *Pedagogy of the Oppressed* (New York: Herder and Herder, 1971), 34.

20. Greg Dimitriadis, *Performing Identity/Performing Culture: Hip-Hop as Text, Pedagogy, and Lived Practice* (New York: Peter Lang, 2009), 159.

21. Dimitriadis, *Performing Identity/Performing Culture*

22. Dimitriadis, *Performing Identity/Performing Culture*, 3.

23. Marc Lamont Hill, *Beats, Rhymes, and Classroom Life: Hip-Hop Pedagogy and the Politics of Identity* (New York: Teachers College Press, 2009), 15.

24. Hill, *Beats, Rhymes, and Classroom Life*, 65.

25. Hill, *Beats, Rhymes, and Classroom Life*, 121.

26. Hill, *Beats, Rhymes, and Classroom Life*, 96.

27. Hill, *Beats, Rhymes, and Classroom Life*, 124.

28. Hill, *Beats, Rhymes, and Classroom Life*.

# (6)

# FLIP-HOP EDUCATION

More overtly than ever, the nature of genius . . . has become an issue bound up with the economic fortunes of nations. Amid the vast modern network of universities, corporate laboratories, and national science foundations has arisen an awareness that the best financed and best organized of research enterprises have not learned to engender, perhaps not even to recognize, world-turning originality.

—James Gleick

The possibilities are numerous once we decide to act and not react.

—George Bernard Shaw

So what is the future of Hip Hop Genius? Will the ideas and practices that have been brewing at the High School for Recording Arts (HSRA) over the past decade penetrate the education mainstream? These questions must be considered on multiple fronts.

On the theoretical tip: Will hip-hop education practitioners and scholars continue to focus primarily on what occurs inside classrooms in traditionally structured schools or will the conversation expand to imagining new kinds of educational programs and leadership?

And on a practical level: Can HSRA continue to offer such an unconventional diploma-granting program in an age of increasing standardization and decreasing state education budgets? If so, will it always be a small anomaly in St. Paul, Minnesota, or will its sphere of influence grow?

This chapter explores a few of the ways that HSRA might play a direct role in spreading Hip Hop Genius sensibilities throughout the field of education and beyond. Beginning by describing the interest the leaders of HSRA have in expanding the school's impact, the chapter goes on to weigh the merits and challenges of attempting to replicate the school in other locations, consider the possibility of establishing the existing program as a lab school to accommodate and acculturate visitors, and highlight the school's potential as a source of inspiration. The chapter concludes by contemplating the broader implications of Hip Hop Genius and suggesting the benefits such a concept could have outside the purview of the education system.

## INCREASING IMPACT

Despite the challenges that HSRA has faced locally as described in chapter 4, the school's successes have been lauded around the country and internationally. Staff and students have presented in settings from open houses to Oxford, and the school has been featured in several articles and short films.

HSRA is one of twenty-four "mentor schools" for the Coalition of Essential Schools, a national network of six hundred small schools that strive to be "personalized, equitable and intellectually challenging."[1] HSRA's role as a mentor school has involved hosting visitors and leading sessions at national conferences.

HSRA has also been a model school for the EdVisions network. EdVisions is an education development organization based in Minnesota. In 2000, EdVisions received a grant from the Bill & Melinda Gates Foundation to develop a cohort of small, project-based schools.

In developing their network, EdVisions embraced HSRA as one of their schools. EdVisions has several successful schools to show visitors, but HSRA demonstrates the success of EdVisions's design principles with urban students of color. When EdVisions has needed to demonstrate the potential of its model for this population, they have brought visitors to HSRA.

In the last decade, educators, nonprofit administrators, and foundation program officers have invested significant time and money in exploring the possibility of replicating successful school designs. Organizations like EdVisions, Big Picture Learning, Communities in Schools, Diploma Plus, Gateway to College, Knowledge Is Power Program (commonly known as KIPP), Street Schools Network, and YouthBuild USA have launched national replication projects. Others, such as the Association for the Advancement of Mexican Americans, Good Shepherd Services, Green Dot Public Schools, High Tech High, and the See Forever Foundation have embarked on regional or local replication efforts.

The leaders at HSRA have decided to explore this possibility as well. A large part of the reason they became interested in expanding their work is the demand they have had for it. In addition to guests who come through EdVisions and the Coalition of Essential Schools, educators from around the country visit to learn from the school. Others invite HSRA's founder David "TC" Ellis and director of development Tony Simmons to speak to and coach school staffs and consult in the development of new schools and programs.

While HSRA is proud to be a part of these networks, the school's leaders feel that over the years they have developed their own unique brand of school. What's more, they believe the design they have developed could make the difference between dropping out and success for many more young people across the country. The question the leadership of HSRA has been asking themselves is, how can they most effectively share and spread what they have built in St. Paul?


## REPLICATING A SCHOOL'S DESIGN

In 2007, Dr. Jennifer Murphy, the program director of Centinela Media Arts Academy in southwestern Los Angeles County, California, learned about HSRA and felt such a program would be the perfect direction for her urban media arts school. Dr. Murphy worked with Ellis and Simmons to structure an agreement through which Studio 4, the education management and studio services company that provides the programmatic backbone for HSRA, would branch out to work with Centinela Media Arts Academy to transform it into the High School for Recording Arts Los Angeles (HSRA LA).

Studio 4 provided materials and coaching for the Centinela Media Arts Academy staff. Ellis and Simmons personally travelled to Los Angeles many times to work with the school's leadership. HSRA Minnesota's studio director, Phil Winden, moved to Los Angeles to build the school's recording studio and to develop the music-engineering program.

The physical layout of the school was arranged to reproduce elements of HSRA Minnesota's design. There was a large open workspace divided with half walls into advisory areas. Posters of the HSRA validations and principles were hung about the room, as were graffiti-style murals. The media lab upstairs was lined with computers stocked with music production and graphic design software. And, of course, there was a state-of-the-art recording studio.

The school's program also followed HSRA Minnesota's design. Students were grouped in advisories and learned through projects and workshops; credits were awarded based on validations; students earned All Access passes, which granted them entry to the school's recording studio; on Wednesdays they held community meetings and on Fridays they had Pick Me Ups.[2]

The first year of the Media Arts Academy/Studio 4 partnership was promising. Students demonstrated their appreciation for the program through consistent attendance and the passion with which they spoke about the school. "[In traditional schools] people looked at me like a low-life gangster," a student named Giovanna Zepeda said. "When I got to Media Arts Academy, they looked at me different, they looked at me like I was somebody. . . . This is the only place we can be ourselves and express ourselves."[3]

There would not be a chance to find out how successful the program could become. A bureaucratic technicality placed the school's future in jeopardy.

The school's charter application renewal date was listed differently in two documents. Murphy was basing her understanding on language in the school's charter, which indicated that there was another year before the charter would have to be renewed. The Centinela Valley Union School District was going by a different date, which they had specified in their resolution to approve the charter. While most districts send notice to schools a year before their charter expires, the Centinela Valley district did not provide any warning or notification to the school until after this expiration date had passed.[4]

There was speculation among charter school advocates that the technicality which threatened the school's future might have been politically and economically motivated. The Centinela Valley district serves as the authorizer for charter schools (though Media Arts was the only one they had ever approved), but the district is also in direct competition with charters for students—and the funding that follows them.

While one would hope that everyone would have students' best interests at heart, some speculated that the district wanted to close Centinela Media Arts Academy to have access to the funding that was allotted to the students who attended the school. Others questioned whether the school board was prejudiced against Centinela Media Arts Academy because of the school's newfound allegiance to hip-hop culture.

As all this was going down in Southern California, a group of educators a thousand miles north in Portland, Oregon, reached out to Studio 4 to ask for help starting an HSRA-style program for local teenagers. Through a consulting contract, Studio 4 provided technical assistance and materials to the Portland educators as they wrote the application for a charter school. In December of 2009, the Portland School Board unanimously approved the school's charter application and the school is slated to open in the fall of 2011.

Throughout the replication efforts in Los Angeles and Portland, Studio 4 has also been working to open a school in New York City. The leaders of HSRA believe that, as the birthplace of hip-hop, New York is the perfect place for a hip-hop high school.

Simmons is a native New Yorker, and since he moved to Minnesota to work with the school, he has dreamed of bringing HSRA's unique design back to his hometown. HSRA has received planning grants for a New York City school from the Black Alliance for Educational Options Small Schools Project and the New York City Center for Charter School Excellence, and has convened a planning team on the ground in New York.

The e-mails and calls requesting HSRA's style of education continue. In 2009, HSRA got word from a team of educators in Atlanta who had already applied for a charter to open a high school based on the HSRA design. Educators who run two successful schools in Baton Rouge have expressed interest in bringing the design to their area.

Replication is an extremely challenging undertaking, but its potential impact makes it tempting. Any school that HSRA helps to open would be able to serve a few hundred students every year, providing them with an educational experience and path to graduation that otherwise would not have been available. For students who have been kicked out or have slid out of all other available options, this could be their only chance at receiving a high school diploma.

Though in the current funding climate and standards-based culture, it would be extremely difficult to support a network of multiple schools like HSRA, if it came to a point where there were a handful of HSRA-style schools spread out around the country that were showing significant signs of success in student retention and achievement, it is possible more would follow. Not enough programs have triumphant track records serving young people who have dropped out and been pushed out of other schools. To the extent that HSRA establishes itself as a proven and replicable design, many more communities could request similar programs.

A small thriving network of schools would put HSRA in a better position to influence national dialogues in both education and hip-hop circles. While successfully developing and running one school for over a decade is significant, demonstrating a distinctive school design's efficacy at a larger scale attracts more attention and inspires different levels of conversations. It compels educational theorists to contemplate the effectiveness of the schools' approach. It pushes funders who are committed to reducing the opportunity gap to consider supporting the development of such programs. It challenges heads from within the hip-hop industry and its fan base to reimagine what it means to be *hip-hop*, and it provokes a reconsideration of the power that the music and culture possess.

Successful replication of the HSRA design would have the potential to have a ripple effect on education. If schools can carry out a high-quality implementation of HSRA's school design and principles, the effect will be broader than just the students they are able to serve. Other schools in their geographic areas can be influenced by their successes and may try implementing elements of the school's design.

Whatever proven successes the HSRA schools can boast will help create political cover for nearby schools to follow in their footsteps in the celebration of hip-hop culture and young peoples' intelligence and abilities, and in the areas of project-based learning, performance-based assessment, and culturally relevant instruction.

The other ripple of influence that a national network of HSRA schools could have would come from the schools' graduates. Having experienced racism, classism, and a range of other structural shorts, many of these young people have had an inside perspective on society's worst problems.

By the time they emerge from HSRA with diplomas, graduates have had the chance to identify and pursue their own passions, they have been responsible for the production of professional-quality products, and they have tasted the powerful positive impact they can have on the world. This boost in skills, self-confidence, and hope, combined with intimate knowledge of society's shortcomings, is powerful.

Some alumni will go on to pursue careers in music like Young Menace, who, as mentioned in chapter 1, produces for several television networks, and Beatnick who—along with his partner K-Salaam—has produced tracks for reggae, dancehall, R&B, and hip-hop artists, such as Buju Banton, Dead Prez, Sizzla, Talib Kweli, Trey Songz, and Young Buck.

Other alumni will make an impact in the field of education. Like the many alum-employees mentioned in earlier chapters, future graduates may work for HSRA or other schools like it. And, as Codie Wilson expressed an interest in doing in chapter 3, some will endeavor to start their own schools or youth programs.

Still others will carry these attributes to other industries, taking the spark of inspiration from attending a school so different from the traditional paradigm and running with it. The more HSRA schools there are around the country, the more graduates will bring this unique blend of self-confidence, skills, and inspiration to external communities. This could be the most powerful impact of replicating HSRA's model.

But maybe none of this will happen through bringing HSRA-style schools to more cities. Replication is a grueling endeavor—one that, if educators are not careful, can pull them away from what they do best: running a great school. It demands immense capacity.

For every day that Ellis, Simmons, and Winden were in Los Angeles, Portland, Atlanta, or New York City, they were not in St. Paul. HSRA has twelve strong years to build on, so it will not fall apart if some of its leaders are away from time to time, but even the best schools are fragile. Removing leaders—or just distracting them—can take a toll.

There is also a danger, whenever a school's design is replicated, that the original model can be copied too literally. A solution that works in one community doesn't necessarily work in another.

This is why High Tech High founder Larry Rosenstock keeps a definition of the word "model" on a scrap of paper stuck to his computer monitor: "Model: a non-functioning replica." Over the years, Rosenstock, who has led a few different approaches to replicating High Tech High's school design—which he intentionally no longer refers to as a "model"—has come to understand that schools are living organisms. Given the right set of conditions, they can spawn new, highly successful sibling schools, but they cannot be cloned.

A large part of HSRA's success is the swagger and agility with which Ellis and his colleagues govern the school. If there is a good idea—like starting the school day at 10 a.m.—even if it is unconventional, they will try it. But what about a school leader who is running HSRA Gotham? What if she has an idea for how to change the program? Can she go ahead and make that change or would it then no longer be an HSRA school?

It would be in the Hip Hop Genius ethos to allow extreme flexibility for change. But what if she made another substantive change? And then another? Eventually the school might look nothing like HSRA. Students might wear uniforms and sit in rows in traditional classes. There might no longer be recording studios. Everything that makes HSRA unique might be gone.

This metamorphosis may sound unlikely—why would someone go to the trouble to start a new school based on an existing school's design, only to change it so dramatically? Yet this has happened to other alternative schools that have tried to replicate.

In fact, the myriad forces that tug schools toward conventional practices can be overwhelming. Even after decades of experience in the field and possessing celebrity education reformer status, Dennis Littky and Elliot Washor felt the powerful pull toward the traditional when they began the Big Picture network of schools. In response to these pressures, in their early years they sported T-shirts emblazoned with the mantra "No Backsliding."

The backslide can happen for many reasons. Sometimes the inspirational leader who has a passion for the alternative design leaves (or is ousted). Other times, new school leaders like the *ideas* of the design in theory, but later they discover that they do not like what these ideas look like in *practice*.

School districts can put tremendous pressure on school leaders to move their designs toward the middle—that is, away from the most edgy and innovative. Or, in some cases, everyone supports the design, but school staff members just don't have the experience, training, or instincts needed to implement it.

For all of the reasons stated above, the balance between maintaining fidelity to essential elements of a school's design and allowing leaders the flexibility to riff on the design is a tricky one. HSRA is in an experimental phase. The school's leaders are testing approaches to replication and trying different levels of involvement in schools that are fashioning themselves in HSRA's image. They may decide to be highly proactive in the replication of HSRA or they may opt for a different approach to creating influence.

## AN OPEN SOURCE LAB SCHOOL

Another way HSRA's leaders could pursue sharing their successes with the world would be to focus on their flagship school. Rather than spending energy helping people in other cities launch hip-hop high schools, they could focus all of their efforts on advancing and articulating the program in St. Paul. Running one phenomenal program could ultimately be their most effective avenue of influence.

If HSRA's leaders double down on innovating within the context of one small school that is already up and running, they will be able to tighten elements of the program and continue the types of creative interventions for which they are known. Further, they could focus on

developing materials that document their innovative educational methods, and they could prepare their students, staff, and facility to host
visitors on a regular basis.

This approach would allow them to build and share expertise in a different manner. It would also serve as inspiration to all who are attracted
to what they are doing and it would bolster their reputation, thereby
amplifying their voice in national dialogues.

Other schools have taken this approach. After ten years of outstand-
ing results helping middle and high school students become the first
members of their families to attend college, the University Park Campus
School in Worcester, Massachusetts, partnered with Jobs for the Future
and Clark University to open the University Park Campus School Institute for Student Success.

Seven times throughout the school year, the institute offers a two-
and-a-half-day training for school developers and leaders. Attendees are
exposed to the University Park Campus School's culture and program
design through immersion in the regular activities of the school. Participants have the chance to observe classes, talk with students, meet
the principal, and attend leadership and instructional workshops. They
then participate in guided opportunities to process and debrief their
experiences.

Similarly, Good Shepherd Services in New York City has been developing and enacting a strategy to share their successes. Good Shepherd Services operates a "Learning Lab" out of the South Brooklyn
Community High School. About twenty visitors each month have the
chance to receive a tour from a current student at the school, observe
classes, listen to an overview of the school's design, receive materials,
and debrief their experiences. Good Shepherd Services has codified
their best practices in a 115-page manual, which they offer for free on
their website.[5]

While University Park and Good Shepherd Services built training
opportunities around successful schools, the Eagle Rock School and
Professional Development Center in Estes Park, Colorado, was, from
its founding in 1991, deliberately intended to be both a school for
young people who had "not experienced success in traditional academic
programs" *and* a professional development center for aspiring and established educators.[6]

People are invited to visit the school through a wide variety of options, including tours, residencies, fellowships, student teaching, and research residencies. Eagle Rock's students and staff also travel to present at conferences and to assist in school reform efforts. Two books and a DVD about Eagle Rock provide additional opportunities for the public to learn about the school.

Like University Park, Good Shepherd Services, and Eagle Rock, HSRA could focus its efforts on developing programming and materials to share with people who visit their school and website. Rather than attempting to manage a replication process, the school's leaders could instead concentrate on making their school as excellent as possible in every area, and then create channels for others to borrow, adapt, sample, and remix elements of their design.

## SERVING AS AN INSPIRATIONAL BURST

HSRA's existence is improbable. Who would have thought that the art and style of poor teenagers in New York City several decades ago would be the basis for a school in Minnesota? And when David Ellis dropped out of high school and was messing with drugs, who would have predicted that he would found such a program? The fact that the school has continued to persevere, grow, and gain momentum for over a decade only adds to its power as a beacon for people who have held little hope for public education.

Hearing Ellis speak about the genesis of the school can inspire people to think differently about what is possible in the field of education. Talking with students about the difference attending HSRA has made in their lives can do the same. The bold and unconventional approach the school has taken to helping students learn, graduate, and succeed beyond high school can replenish people's gusto for thinking and acting outside the box.

This sort of inspirational burst may be HSRA's most effective tool in changing the experiences for students in large public schools. It is unlikely that the administration of such schools would approach HSRA with a desire to adopt the school's design. It's hard to imagine how they would even implement the HSRA model at such a large scale. But individual teachers or administrators could still find inspiration in the radical approach that HSRA has taken as an institution.

Also, hip-hop artists and fans who hear Ellis's story could become inspired to enter the field of education. The fact that Ellis was not formally trained as an educator yet has managed to do so much in the field might inspire others to try similar endeavors in the education space or in other social sectors. Ellis's story could have a similar effect for people who don't identify with hip-hop but relate to his struggles as a young man with the education system, drugs, and finding a productive role in society.

HSRA's innovative spirit inspires people beyond the field of education. Susan Campion, a business consultant and instructor at the Center for Business Excellence at the University of St. Thomas, recently presented about HSRA at a Global Leadership Conference in Prague.

Campion's workshop, entitled "Beats, Rhymes and Breakthrough Ideas: Lessons in Innovation from Hip Hop High," drew messages for businesspeople from the work of the students and staff of HSRA. Others outside of the education field have and will continue to learn from and be inspired by HSRA's innovative and entrepreneurial spirit and actions.

After all, HSRA's existence and practices exemplify exactly what our education system and our planet need right now: creative and audacious solutions to massive problems. The current secretary of education, Arne Duncan, recognizes this need and uses the term "innovation" frequently. His department has recently launched a $650-million Investing in Innovation Fund.

In order to apply, programs must have "demonstrated success in significantly increasing student academic achievement for all groups of students."[7] In other words, the fund will support organizations that have successfully run a program for long enough that they have had time to measure its effectiveness—undoubtedly great work to sponsor, but perhaps not a true boost to innovation.[8]

A more direct investment in innovation would be awarding grants to programs that were setting out to try new things; initiatives that had not demonstrated success yet but were good ideas with good people behind them. There would have to be a built-in tolerance for the unknown, for failure—or, at least, for unexpected results. This would be a risky move for the federal government to make, but it would encourage dramatic and profound discoveries, as opposed to incremental change.

Regardless of federal support, real innovation will occur in the education sector.

Consider the hip-hop industry. Major record labels keep serving up the same formula: misogynist, hypercapitalist, super-gangster lyrics over beats by the producer du jour. But there are increasingly large amounts of good, genre-boundary-defying music being made. It is just being released on independent labels, more likely to be sold on the Internet than at the record store. This is not to belittle the challenges faced by independent artists. Rather, it is to point out that there are always channels, literal and figurative, through which cutting-edge music can be heard. HSRA's songs and stories of success can provide voices of inspiration—theme music for the changes to come.

## THE FUTURE OF EDUCATION

Blending multiple elements, flipping their original uses and meanings, and creating some newness—education must continue in the spirit of hybridization and innovation exemplified by hip-hop.

Evolving manifestations of social justice education, media literacy, and identity development are crucial parts of this, but there are countless additional opportunities to reconsider educational experiences at every level, from individual interactions to the very structure of the institutions in which those interactions take place. Traditional schooling and even many iterations of hip-hop education are not designed to fully honor and engage students' brilliance in all the diverse and sometimes contradictory ways it can occur.

Whether students are weaving clever wordplay into their writing, blinging out the rims of their bike with tin foil, or starting up a natural soda business, educators must encourage, extend, and learn from students' ingenuity and resourcefulness. This cannot happen in a reality confined by rows of desks, textbooks, lockers, and bells that ring every forty-five minutes—even if during those periods the desks are pulled into circles and the textbooks are replaced with the hippest hip-hop workbooks.

When hip-hop educators began bringing hip-hop texts into schools, most did not have much power or validation. They were visiting artists, teachers' assistants, student teachers, and new teachers. They did not have a body of scholarly work supporting their efforts. But times have changed.

There are annual conferences about hip-hop education. Research studies have been conducted and books have been written. New York University has launched a Hip Hop Education Center for Research, Evaluation, and Professional Development. And, perhaps most importantly, many hip-hop educators have gained power within their schools.

Teachers' assistants have become teachers, and teachers have become principals. Others have moved from the schoolhouse to district-level employment, education nonprofit organizations, and academia. College students writing essays about hip-hop for undergraduate education courses have become tenured faculty members. This means that, collectively, hip-hop educators are in a position to consider different, bolder levels of hip-hop education.

The time has come to follow HSRA's lead in breaking the elements of schools into pieces, reconfiguring and reassembling them, just as a hip-hop producer patches together segments of songs to construct a new musical composition. Most good hip-hop beats don't consist of samples from just one song. Similarly, as HSRA has demonstrated, a hip-hop school can pull from a diverse array of sources, fading between techniques, and occasionally speeding one up or pulling it backwards to concoct something no one previously knew was possible.

"Struggle breeds creativity," graffiti legend Doze says, articulating a belief shared by many in the hip-hop community and beyond. "We've got it good in America, so maybe that's why hip-hop is so fucked up, 'cause we got it so *good* now."[9]

Doze's statement about hip-hop could apply to the education system or to the nation more generally. This country's ethos of abundance has led to some lazy habits. But there are urgent battles afoot. Needs for ingenuity now come in other forms: the energy crisis, unemployment, keeping communities safe without incarcerating millions of people, keeping our country safe without fighting wars.

Underlying all of these challenges is the need to improve the education system, which despite millions of intelligent, caring people dedicating their lives to it, is losing far too many students and failing to prepare many others for the struggles ahead.

Whether you view it as music, a movement, or a mind-set, it would be unfair to expect hip-hop to solve any of the problems listed above. Yet it would be a mistake to ignore its resourceful reflexes: creativity, collage, collaboration.

Had the New York City Sanitation Department been more diligent about trash collection in low-income neighborhoods, breakdance moves like the windmill and the headspin might never have been invented. But because in the 1970s countless families chose to replace their linoleum floors from the previous decades, and because all of this linoleum was left in the trash along with copious amounts of cardboard, b-boys and b-girls discovered a new surface to dance on, and invented new moves to maximize its potential.[10]

Parents' trash was children's treasure. The city's neglect was irresponsible, but in its negligence young geniuses sweated out possibility.

There are too many problems to solve, yet our society is dancing around so many wasted resources. What refuse could we be dancing *on*? And what are the new moves? Whether hip-hop continues to be a dominant cultural force or fades, the instincts, ingenuity, and swagger must continue—in honor of all of the geniuses who have come before, for all of the geniuses to be.

## NOTES

1. Coalition of Essential Schools, "About the Coalition of Essential Schools," http://www.essentialschools.org/items (accessed December 17, 2010).

2. See chapters 1 and 2 for descriptions of community meetings and Pick Me Ups.

3. Mitchell Landsberg, "Hip Hop High Loses Its Charter," *Los Angeles Times*, July 10, 2008, http://articles.latimes.com/2008/jul/10/local/me-hiphop10 (accessed December 17, 2010).

4. Ibid, http://articles.latimes.com/2008/jul/10/local/me-hiphop10/2.

5. The Good Shepherd Services manual can be found at: http://www.goodshepherds.org/programs/community/transfer-schools/replication.html (accessed December 17, 2010).

6. Eagle Rock School and Professional Development Center, "Quick Facts," http://www.eaglerockschool.org/about_us/quick_facts.asp (accessed December 17, 2010).

7. U.S. Department of Education, "Investing in Innovation Fund (I3) Eligibility Criteria," *Ed.gov*, http://www2.ed.gov/programs/innovation/eligibility.html (accessed December 17, 2010).

8. There is a bottom level of grants in the Investing in Innovation Fund for "Development grants," which require less preexisting proof of success, but Duncan makes clear in the U.S. Department of Education's press release "Secretary Duncan Releases Application for $650 Million to Support Innovation" on March 8, 2010: "This fund awards three different grants to programs at three different stages of development that all share one thing in common—evidence of success." The press release can be found at *Ed.gov*, http://www2.ed.gov/news/pressreleases/2010/03/03082010.html (accessed December 17, 2010).

9. Jeff Chang, "Codes and the B-Boy's Stigmata: An Interview with Doze," in *Total Chaos: The Art and Aesthetics of Hip-Hop*, ed. Jeff Chang (New York: Basic Civitas, 2006), 319.

10. Danny Hoch, "Toward a Hip-Hop Aesthetic: A Manifesto for the Hip-Hop Arts Movement," in Chang, *Total Chaos*, 353.

# A NOTE FROM/
# ABOUT THE AUTHOR

One day in 2004, a crew of out-of-towners rolled into the converted garage that housed the youth program I directed on the south side of Providence, Rhode Island. The small group of teenage and adult visitors was from the Midwest and, while in the area to attend a conference, had been told to check out our program—the AS220 Broad Street Studio.

Youth staff members gave them a tour of our hip-hop recording studio; showed them the murals, photographs, magazines, and apparel being produced; and explained our mission to serve as an incubator for young artists and leaders, especially those in and transitioning out of juvenile prison, group homes, and foster care.

Our guests told us a bit about the school they came from, which sounded very similar to our organization, except that they had figured out how to infuse a diploma-granting academic curriculum.

I didn't learn more about their school until a few years later, when I began working for the Alternative High School Initiative, a national network of organizations replicating innovative schools.[1] One of my responsibilities was to make site visits to schools that were members of the initiative.

Our midwestern visitors' school, the High School for Recording Arts (HSRA), was one of the first that I saw. On that trip I found a community that was merging the creative youth empowerment work that we engaged in at AS220 Broad Street Studio with an academic program reflective of best practices in alternative education.

I was struck by HSRA. It was unlike anything I had ever seen. A group of us in Providence had struggled to build a space where young people could be themselves, rep their cultures, broadcast their voices, and have agency in the governance of the program. And I had attended, worked in, and visited schools that engaged students through alternative methods.

But I had never seen a place that did both, especially—though by no means exclusively—for black students. What captivated me about HSRA was that not only did the culture and atmosphere mirror students' interests, identities, and instincts, but so did the curriculum.

Since that first visit, I have engaged with the school in several capacities. I have worked on coordinating a national conference that featured a visit to the school; attended events with HSRA students and staff in Atlanta, Los Angeles, New York, New Jersey, Philadelphia, and San Francisco; brokered relationships between the school and national youth programs; facilitated professional development workshops for staff members; and spoken publicly about the school at events across the country.

When the leaders of the school and I agreed that I would write this book, I moved to Minnesota, lived in Minneapolis for a year and a half, and spent more than one hundred hours in the school, observing and engaging with students and staff.

This is not an objective study. I came to this project a proponent of the ideas and a friend of the people discussed herein. I also came with the agenda of identifying and explaining the elements of Hip Hop Genius as they are operationalized in an existing institution. To this end, I did not describe everything about HSRA the way I might have if I had set out to write a portrait of a school. I focused on highlighting aspects of the school's program that I believed would push public dialogue about the possibilities that lie waiting in the intersections of hip-hop and education.

That said, I have made every effort to be precise in my descriptions, claims, and conclusions. My goal is not to place the subjects on a pedestal from which they cannot move, morph, or grow. Rather, I hope that by dedicating these pages to describing HSRA's history and programs and defining Hip Hop Genius, I can advance conversations that will ultimately bring greater attention, including both accolades and constructive criticism, to the school and the concept.

Since this book is about the powerful potential of merging hip-hop and education, I wrote it in a hybrid language. I hope my hip-hop family is patient with any words that are specific to the education genre and that my fellow educators hang in with the hip-hop slang and quotes that are woven throughout. In some ways, the words and concepts with which we are least familiar offer the greatest opportunities for learning.

I intentionally have written very little about myself in the preceding chapters. In these final few pages, I intend to share a bit of who I am, my relationship to hip-hop education and the High School for Recording Arts, what motivated me to write a book about Hip Hop Genius, and my choices regarding narrative style.

This book emerged from a collective effort. As explained in the introduction, the concept of Hip Hop Genius was generated in fellowship with several other educators. Similarly, many of the ideas presented in the preceding pages were developed through our communal conversations.

When I began writing, I was not sure whether I would ultimately be the solo author, so it made sense to compose in the third person. Even once it became clear that I would complete the manuscript alone, I decided not to insert myself as a character beyond the introduction both for the practical reasons described above and for the ideological reasons that follow.

On a conceptual level, Hip Hop Genius has become a mantra for us, and for a growing group of educators who have joined us. We have become an informal think tank with the goals of advancing the ideas described in this book and housing resources to enable the development of schools and organizations that support the brilliance of young people.

Rather than establishing a stringent set of criteria for Hip Hop Genius schools or educational practices, the intention is to engender global dialogue about the importance of recognizing and supporting resourceful ingenuity, particularly in students who have been scapegoated by society.

Our hope is that by codifying these concepts and serving as a repository for relevant resources, we can inspire individuals who, whether formally trained as educators or not, have the potential to bring empowering experiences to populations of young people who have been treated as burdens, liabilities, and criminals. With the right spark and support, these young people can become change agents—leaders in positive systemic change, by whatever means are most transformative.

No formal think tank or organization is needed. The spirit of Hip Hop Genius can be embodied and built upon anywhere.

Hopefully this book can be a part of the process. The intention is not to over-romanticize a complex culture or encourage uncritical duplication of a particular institution but rather to inspire resourcefulness and innovation in education and all walks of life. Because this book has a social justice agenda that comes from this collective vision, it did not feel accurate or effective to present it as "Sam's story."

As I corresponded with agents about the idea for this book, I was asked more than once if it could be written in a Jonathan Kozol-esque style. I was told that if I built a dramatic narrative around my experiences at the school it could be "best-seller material."

When done well, a white author's moral outrage—brightened with an appropriate ratio of rays of hope—can indeed become a best-seller. But as the only white member of the Hip Hop Genius collective, I felt uncomfortable inserting myself as a protagonist. This book exists to push conversations about how to creatively change systems and I did not want to occlude the discussion of these ideas with my own moral coming-of-rage story.

Of course, even in absence of personal anecdotes, this book is still informed by my experiences and perspectives. I am not an impartial researcher who dispassionately selected hip-hop education as a subject of study.

I was raised by educators, studied education history and policy, was certified as a teacher, and have worked with young people my entire career. Growing up in an urban environment in the 1980s and 1990s, hip-hop was cemented as an integral part of my cultural identity long before I ever heard the term "cultural identity." And for years, I have taught hip-hop workshops in elementary, middle schools, high schools, and juvenile prisons.

Whenever I facilitate hip-hop workshops with groups of young people, I like to begin by asking their names and what music they're currently feeling. When they list their favorite artists, I often ask, "Why?"

Almost inevitably, the exact phrase "Because he's real" will be at the top of the list. While beat selection, rhymes, and flow—and increasingly, advertising and cross-branding—all influence which rappers people prefer, another critical piece is who listeners believe an artist to be—in other words, the artist's identity.

Of course, many rappers understand this and, in an effort to please, craft back-stories that are more faithful to the popular "Get Rich or Die Tryin'" narrative than to their own realities.[2] Others shine off the strength of their own personal truth, like a young Common Sense telling listeners that he did not grow up poor and that he worried about his own drinking, when those were far from common things to say.[3] Either way, the point remains: People want to know who's behind the curtain, and this information affects their interpretation and reception of the product.

When it comes to writing on hip-hop education, heads want to know: Is this cat who's writing a book about hip-hop education *hip-hop*? Does he understand the history and the elements of the culture? *Does he live it?* Can he rhyme, b-boy, DJ, or write graffiti? Or does he just talk about it? All of these concerns can be wrapped into one simple three-word question: *Is he real?*

My first instinct could be to respond to such questions as if someone just disrespected me in a freestyle battle. But I want to put my hip-hop bravado in check and tell you how real and not-real I am, so that you have a sense of where I am coming from and so that ambiguities and speculations don't cloud your interpretations of this book.

Despite trying hard as a seven year old, I was a terrible b-boy, graffiti artist, DJ, and emcee. I gave up the dancing first—pretty much as soon as I started (I had rhythm and coordination—just not both at once!). I continued to mess with graffiti through my middle school skateboard phase and into my teenage years (mostly just as a lookout for my far-more-talented friends).

As a freshman in high school, I inherited two record players and a mixer and made a lot of mixtapes. Throughout college, I DJed parties, co-hosted a hip-hop radio show, and co-directed the hip-hop department at the station. I've never been a skilled turntablist, but I have always enjoyed selecting music that moves the crowd—on the dance floor and emotionally.

My love of emceeing began in the middle of the 1980s with my brothers and a tape recorder. First, we rapped along with Melle Mel to "The Message" and the "Beat Street Breakdown." Then we recorded our first track, "The Ewok Rap."

In high school, I began freestyling and fell in love with the fast-paced improvisational creativity it demanded. After graduating I began recording a lot more and occasionally performing locally. A compilation that I had a song on sold some copies in France, but that was the height of my fame. I never put any energy into making a career out of making music. It just was and is something I love to do.

Much of my successful teaching and work with young people has been based around hip-hop music. This was not an intentional choice I made at the beginning of my career as an educator. It is something that emerged naturally. I love to rap and talk about hip-hop music, and so do a lot of students. Others enjoy listening, critiquing, and making beats.

When teaching social studies, students and I have analyzed the commentary in relevant rap songs. When teaching language arts, we have looked at the compositional techniques and poetic devices at play in rap music. When helping young people stay out of prison, the opportunity to record and perform has served as a motivating factor.

For students in prison or feeling trapped in their environs, freestyling and writing rhymes can be a powerful channel for self-expression, the exploration of fantasies, and the development of societal critiques. As poet Jimmy Santiago Baca who taught himself to read and write in prison explains, "Through language I was free. I could respond, escape, indulge; embrace or reject earth or the cosmos. I was launched on an endless journey without boundaries or rules, in which I could salvage the floating fragments of my past, or be born anew in the spontaneous ignition of understanding some heretofore concealed aspect of myself."[4]

Over the years, students have expressed similar sentiments, and Baca's description resonates with my own relationship to the act of selecting and arranging words.

One of the most effective elements in my interactions with young people has been my willingness to do this spontaneously. The rawness and unpredictability of a teacher or youth program director freestyling grabs and hold students' attention. It demonstrates a willingness to be vulnerable in front of them.

At its essence, freestyling works when an emcee taps into her or his soul and lets it flow out in rhyme. Though I rarely freestyle these days, for many years composing free associations aloud in front of students allowed me to get closer to answering the perennial questions about my realness.

In addition to how deeply immersed one is in hip-hop culture, another issue of authenticity arises around whether an emcee or author has really experienced the harsh urban realities that they are rapping or, in this case, writing about. Like Common Sense, I did not grow up poor. My parents made living wages as teachers and eventually transitioned into work in higher education and nonprofit organizations. There was not a bunch of surplus money hanging around, but there was never a lack of food on the table.

There was, however, a lot of other privilege flowing through my upbringing. My grandfather was a doctor. His financial success allowed us to spend summers on Cape Cod. All four of the adults in the house I grew up in were college educated. Three are published authors. Two are bilingual.

I grew up in North Cambridge, Massachusetts, a racially and socioeconomically diverse urban environment. I lived a few blocks from low-income housing towers, which featured prominently in the view from my bedroom window and in my childhood understanding of the universe in which I existed.

As a kid, I saw how poverty affected families. So, even though he intended it in a derogatory way, when Jay-Z rapped to Nas, "You ain't live it, you witnessed it from your folks' pad," it resonated with me.[5]

I didn't live it. It wasn't me walking down the street with the ghetto blaster on my shoulder bumping the hottest new songs. It wasn't me getting harassed by the cops or stabbed at Popeye's. But on warm nights I would press my face against the screen window of my third-story room to see if I could find the sources of the music, shouting, and occasional gunshots, and the next day on the bus to my alternative public school I'd hear stories about what went down.

I have continued to live in similar neighborhoods and when I got too old to attend diverse urban alternative schools, I began working at them. Through each of these experiences, I have been one of the most privileged members of these communities.

I am a white, heterosexual man with a degree from an Ivy League institution. While I do not come from the wealthiest family or an Aryan background (as a Jew, I have a heritage of persecution, despite the current ruling class's embrace of my garbanzo complexion), I have pounds of privilege and access that are systematically denied to the groups of young people who created the culture and are enrolled in the school that comprise the major focal points of this book.

Some of those young people will undoubtedly write books that better address the topics touched upon in this volume. I humbly offer this as an interim text. My beliefs, ideas, weaknesses, fears, sense of humor, and passion are, of course, present throughout. I am proud of these qualities as they help illuminate new understandings and I apologize for the moments in which they cloud the brilliant subject matter.

## NOTES

1. The Alternative High School Initiative is now known as the Association for High School Innovation (AHSI).

2. "Get Rich or Die Tryin'" is the name of 50 Cent's debut album and also a mantra for some members of the hip-hop generation (as well as capitalists of all ages).

3. Lonnie Rashied Lynn Jr., aka Common Sense, "Rich Man vs. Poor Man," *Resurrection*, Relativity Records, 1994, compact disc.

4. Jimmy Santiago Baca, "Coming into Language," in *Doing Time: 25 Years of Prison Writing*, ed. Bell Gale Chevigny (New York: Arcade, 2000), 103.

5. Shawn C. Carter, "Takeover," *The Blueprint*, Roc-A-Fella/Def Jam, 2001, compact disc.

# INDEX

# ACKNOWLEDGMENTS

First and foremost, I am grateful to all of the young people who have attended the High School for Recording Arts. Without you all, the stories in this book would not exist—and without your openness, I wouldn't know or be able to tell them.

I deeply appreciate everyone who helped create this book by giving feedback on drafts of the manuscript, including experts on the subject matter, High School for Recording Arts leaders and staff members— David "TC" Ellis, Tony Simmons, Kowanna Powell Anderson, Mike Conway, Darlene Leiding, and Barbara Murphy; brothers—Gregory Falk Cluster, Adam Steinberg Seidel, and Isaac Ewell; sister—Savannah Shange; parents—Adria Steinberg, Steve Seidel, Nancy Falk, and Dicky Cluster; mentors—Joy James, Herb Kohl, Elliot Washor, Charlie Mojkowski, and Kathleen Cushman; hip-hop education colleagues— Michael Cirelli, Chelsea Gregory, and Marcella Runell-Hall; friends— Albert Saldana, Adam Reich, and Laura Rubin; and my writing coach extraordinaire—Karen Pittelman. Karen's support, guidance, and sense of humor made the process of writing this book enjoyable. Anyone who needs a coach should work with her: www.writersremedy.com.

There are many other current and past staff members at the High School for Recording Arts who helped make this project possible and a pleasure: Paula Anderson, Bryan Rossi, Saintanne Agbangba, "Big Layne" Bellamy, "Little Layne" Bellamy, The Real Young Bishop, Matthew Brown, Kashta French, Libby Harris, Darryl "Duke" Gibson, Bonnie Hughes, Michelle "Miki Starr" Martin, Jonathan B. Moore, Dario Otero, TeLisa "Taz" Powell, Mandy Smith, Donte "Humble Child" Suttle, Tabitha Wheeler, "Monsta Codie Indiana" Wilson, Phil Winden, Darryl Young . . . and everyone else who has worked at the school over the last few years. Also, friends of the school, who have been friends to this project and me: Susan Campion and Barbara Portnoy.

The notion of "Hip Hop Genius" would not exist if Isaac Ewell had not brought together David "TC" Ellis, Tony Simmons, Jason Green, Fanon Che Wilkins, and myself to build about hip-hop education in 2005. Camilla Greene, Lawrence Patrick III, and Chris "Kazi" Rolle have since joined us and contributed to the concept. I'm honored to know and work with this talented and passionate group of educators. Over the past few years, I've had the opportunity to build with additional leaders exploring the intersections of hip-hop and education, including Martha Diaz and her crew at NYU, Robert Rivera, Chris Emdin, Brandon Frame, and my old friend Micah Berkley.

I have had the privilege of learning from some other amazing educators throughout my life, including Bil Johnson, Carlina Rinaldi, Demian Yattaw, Doug Thomas, Elliot Washor, Joan Soble, Joy James, Judy Lazarus, Kanai Sensei, Kathy Greeley, Larry Aaronson, Larry Rosenstock, Michael Eldridge, Peter Hocking, Rick Benjamin, Robert Arellano, Ron Berger, Ross Cheit, Sioux Hall, and Tamara Berman Ishee.

My young mentors—Andre Bradley, Mike Domenech, Shane Lee, Tim Natividad, Albert Saldana, Kariim Sekka, and Chandelle Wilson—have constantly reinforced my deep belief in the brilliance of young people.

Several friends who have been through the process of writing and sharing books with the world have given me great advice throughout this process, including several people mentioned previously, as well as Jamie Schwesnedl, who made moving to Minnesota a holistically enriching experience full of homegrown vegetables, great new friends, hilarious Internet videos, and thoughtful conversations about writing and publishing; Bryant Terry and Billy "Upski" Wimsatt, who shared valuable insights about their journeys as writers committed to social justice; and

Ron Newell, who put me in touch with a publisher who understood the importance of this book's subject matter.

I'm honored that Tom Koerner saw the value of publishing this text and I appreciate the energy he and his colleagues—Lindsey Schauer, Andrew Yoder, Karin Cholak, Sam Caggiula, Kristina Mann, and others—at Rowman & Littlefield have put behind it. Jocelyn Burrell, Alison Harris, and Emily Griffin all helped me to better understand the world of publishing.

I wouldn't understand hip-hop the way I do without all of the artists I've had the honor of collaborating with over the years: Joshua "Plan B" Padilla, Vincent "V-Eye" Wadlington (Rest In Peace), Grim, Jeep Jack, Microft Holmes, Physical, Shareef Jackson, Sammy Bananas Posner, Alumno Martinez, David Gonzalez, Kareem "Bronx Emcee" Caines, Deph Dephiance, DJ Tek, Rascal, L3y8, Alexis D'Boys, Papa Humbertico, Los Aldeanos, Los Paisanos, and Randee Acosta.

Many of the ideas in this book germinated at the AS220 Broad Street Studio and were influenced by the young people and staff there, including several people mentioned above, as well as many others, such as Beast, Harmony Boyce, Kevin "Poet" Carosi, Arlene Chorney, Patrick "Ill Won" Clinton, Bert Crenca, Roger D'Ambra, DNA, Teryl "Bear" Foster, Emil Hciple, Luis Hernandez, Shane Howe, Vernon Knight, Scott Lapham, Ghislaine Jean-Mahone, Merarri McKinney, Nina Memi, Anjel and Amber Newmann, Nisha Purushotham, Adam Reich, the Rezendes boys, Jeremy "Suave" Richardson, Laura Rubin, Heidy Soares, Twiggz, Bob Watson, Wyzdom, Young Playa, Zipper, and Gaby Mollinedo (who designed the cover of this book!). Big shouts to all the current AS220 Youth heads!

Colleagues from the Alternative High School Initiative/the Association for High School Innovation, AS220, Big Picture Learning, the Bill & Melinda Gates Foundation, the Black Alliance for Educational Options, the Criminal Justice Initiative, Diploma Plus, GOOD, the Habla architects, Operation REACH, the Maysles Cinema/Institute, the Providence Youth Arts Collaborative, Resource Generation, and the Rhode Island School of Design have both informed the ideas in this book and been supportive throughout the process of writing it.

For friendship, famship, and support, I thank Gramma May Ruth, Ashley and GG Herring, Terra Goolsby, Rafi Hopkins, Tylea Simone,

Shradha Patel, Natalie Lewis, Adeola Oredola, Simon Moore, Carmen Gill, Shivohn Garcia, Ariana Wohl, the Maysles, Adam and Candice Anitra Manson Weinstock, Eric and Candace Pugatch, Sian Heder and David Newsom, Simon Doolittle and the Jewish Kate Moss, Zoe and Griff Foxley, the Estrins, Kabira Stokes-Hochberg, Molly Hein, Mattie Weiss, Noah Danoff, Courtney Hull, Alejandra Tobar Alatriz, Liana and Michael Krupp, Dina Lopez and Craig Zheng, Miyo Tubridy, Isaac Souweine, Daniel Souweine, Jeff Zimbalist, Jamie Laurie, Peter Hocking, Adam Bush, the College Unbound crew, Anika Vaughn-Cooke, Carolyn Norr, Angela Schwesnedl, Justin Grayson, Tracy Hewat, Gretza Pineiro, Anh Nguyen, Nicholas Reville, Benjamin Wertheimer, James Evrard, Yang Yan, David Lemmel, Jason Yoon, Keith Catone, Dulari Tahbildar, Ianthe Hensman, Leticia Tejada, Lauren Smock-Randall, Maythinee Washington, Clay Rockefeller, Briana Pearson, Bruce Astrein, Anna Pelrine, and so many others who have shown love over the years.

For all of the above and for lifting me up when I literally couldn't stand (it) anymore: Nelson Walker III, Philip Maysles, and Greta Hansen.

The children of friends and colleagues keep me inspired for the next generation: Kingston, Olivia, Che and Marley, Marly Mae, Shaine, Jaiden, Jesina and Maliya, Ella, Luca, Hazel, and Sage and Amari.

To all of the pioneers of hip-hop culture and progressive education, thank you for your generosity and for everything you have shared. I hope this book honors the traditions from which it is born and without which it would not be possible.